Preparing Helping Professionals to Meet Community Needs: Generalizing from the Rural Experience

Edited by

Shirley J. Jones
and
Joan Levy Zlotnik

Council on Social Work Education
Alexandria, Virginia

Library of Congress Cataloging-in-Publication Data

Preparing helping professionals to meet community needs: generalizing from the rural experience / edited by Shirley J. Jones and Joan Levy Zlotnik.
    p. cm.
    Based on papers presented at a focus group meeting held at the Nelson A. Rockefeller Institute for Government, State University of New York at Albany, Oct. 31–Nov. 1, 1996
    Includes bibliographical references.
    ISBN 0-87293-059-9
    1. Social service, Rural–United States–Congresses. 2. Rural health ser-vices–United States–Congresses. 3. Social work education–United States–Congresses. 4. Community and college-education–United States–Congresses. I. Jones, Shirley J., 1931–   . II. Zlotnik, Joan Levy.
    HV91.P73 1998
    361.973′09173′4–dc21   97-53247
                                                CIP

Manufactured in the United States of America.

Table of Contents

Foreword

It was our pleasure to help support the focus group meeting entitled "Professional Development of Helping Professions in Rural Communities," a community–university partnership held at the Nelson A. Rockefeller Institute for Government in Albany, NY, on October 31 and November 1, 1996. We are pleased that funding from the W.K. Kellogg Foundation has made this publication possible. This book encourages helping professions (including, but not limited to, social work and health care) to use interdisciplinary collaboration and partnerships to bring about effective community change. In addition, it challenges educators and others responsible for professional education and development to design curricula to meet the needs of rural and urban communities.

We hope this publication will facilitate further discussion of topics presented at the focus group meeting. The authors have addressed issues that are important as we move into the 21st century. The role of the social worker as an information entrepreneur, perspectives for rural health professionals, attributes of the generalist approach, economic and social development, and collaboration and partnerships are just a few of the areas examined.

We encourage you to use the contents of this book to develop interdisciplinary partnerships and to plan and implement curricula to prepare helping professionals for the future.

Jeanne Gullahorn
Dean in Residence
Council of Graduate Schools
Washington, DC

Donald W. Beless
Executive Director
Council on Social Work Education

Preface

What is the role of the university in preparing "helping professionals" to work in communities, especially rural communities? How can we support collaboration among disciplines in the academy so that they can work effectively in the community? How can we promote community–university partnerships that honor the strengths and values of communities and that capture the expertise universities can offer? What role can students play as bridge builders between the university and the community?

These are some of the critical questions that are addressed in this book. Each chapter provides a snapshot into contemporary efforts to prepare social workers and other helping professionals to build on individual, family, and community strengths and to invigorate the connections between community and economic development and individual and family well-being. It underscores the critical need for collaborative efforts between those in need of services and those who provide service, between universities and communities and across disciplines. The authors build on presentations from a powerful focus group meeting produced by the schools of social welfare, public health, and business at the State University of New York at Albany and the Council on Social Work Education in the fall of 1996. The focus group intended to investigate what the preparation of professionals such as social workers, teachers, nurses, public health specialists, and other helpers in rural communities should look like as we move into the 21st century. It examined many of the questions raised above by gathering community members, representatives of community agencies, national leaders, students, and educators from several disciplines to exchange ideas and explore common goals. The focus group reinforced the importance of empowering the community, developing trusting relationships, listening to the community, and forging partnerships between the community and its professionals.

The W.K. Kellogg Foundation is supporting the publication and dissemination of this material because the information within the chapters will help people in universities, community agencies, national organizations, and foundations. The mission of the foundation is "to help people help themselves through the practical application of knowledge and resources to improve their quality of life and that of future generations." Those who read these pages should profit from them and from efforts by communities and universities and by professionals and community members to work toward individual, family, and community well-being.

Gloria Meert
W.K. Kellogg Foundation
Battle Creek, MI

Introduction

Planning is a development process usually sparked by an instigator —such as a need, dream, tension, conflict, suffering, or flawed policy—or a combination thereof. To accommodate the many sparks that grew into the focus group meeting, Kahn's (1969) social planning framework was used to guide the planning process. The spiral (versus linear) nature of his framework permitted a synergy for collaboration and coordination between the Council on Social Work Education (CSWE) and the State University of New York, University at Albany (SUNYA). The meeting's co-planners entered the project with their own concerns, interests, and values, and they came out with a creative way to investigate the many shared realities of all involved. Although choices had to be made at every level, and often cost and time set priorities, the planning process resulted in opportunities to evaluate, secure feedback, and make changes for a successful program and, now, a collaborative book.

Shirley J. Jones (SUNYA) and Joan Levy Zlotnik (CSWE) were the human instigators of this partnership. While working on student–faculty partnerships and professional development, Jones encountered Zlotnik's research on collaboration and partnerships at CSWE's 1995 Annual Program Meeting. In spring 1996, with a grant from the Office of Research and the School of Social Welfare at SUNYA, Jones's macro social work class designed and held a workshop to promote university–community partnerships; Zlotnik was a guest speaker. Planning for the focus group meeting then moved forward, inspired by the student-sponsored workshop and Jones's (1996) working paper "Collaboration and Coordination regarding Rural Social Work and Economic Development," parts of which are incorporated in Chapter 1 here.

Plan for the Book

This book is intended to provide helping professionals with information that will help them better meet the needs of communities. The chapters use rural communities as case studies and incorporate the strengths, generalist, and systems perspectives, which provide a view for assessing and analyzing complex situations and problems. Rural communities remain the focus, because they offer an opportunity to view dynamic relationships between and within rural and urban areas. They provide manageable situations in which to explore issues such as rapid and unprecedented change, the means to address transition, future roles and responsibilities for helping professionals, the generalist approach to providing services, and the need for continuous professional education and training.

Rural social work also adapts well to the eclectic theoretical base and systems framework of the generalist approach. Generalist social workers can intervene at every level and are guided by a planned change process with problem solving and strengths perspectives (a point made by Anne Fortune at the focus group meeting). For most of the authors here, the generalist perspective begins with a problem solving approach that can be supplemented by other decision making models. For example, by borrowing from a rational approach, with its linear and value-neutral process, practitioners can reach goals in the shortest amount of time and at the least cost. Limitations to this approach (such as applying it to macro-level practice) might be addressed with the nonlinear and value-laden process of the action model, which concentrates on the needs and perceptions of a community (Brueggemann, 1996; Netting, Kettner, & McMurtry, 1993).

Part 1 of the book frames the agenda for rural partnerships. Shirley J. Jones's chapter, "Professional Development in the Human Services: Implications for the 21st Century" questions whether helping professionals are being prepared to address the complex situations and problems of our time. Joan Levy Zlotnik expands on preparation of helping professionals for the future and makes specific recommendations regarding education and training in her chapter, "Preparing Human Service Workers for the 21st Century: A Challenge to Professional Education." A group of social work students (Irene Cody, Kristine Collins, Linda Mokarry, Mark Morris, and Kim Rosenkrans) express concerns about social workers in the 21st century and how the generalist approach can better empower helping professionals. Their chapter is entitled "Social Workers Facing the 21st Century: Are We Ready?"

Part 2 presents rural communities as a case study. Chapter 4, "Rural Health Care: A Challenge for Academic Medical Centers," was written by Henry Pohl, director of the Office of Medical Education and associate dean for medical education at Albany Medical College. Pohl discusses the health needs of rural and urban communities, rural health care initiatives, and university partnerships. Next, Judith and Joseph Davenport, academic and practitioner, respectively, address the generalist approach, community economic development, interdisciplinary collaboration, and professional development in their chapter, "Economic and Social Development and Rural Social Work as a Model of the Generalist Approach for the 21st Century." Judith is director of the School of Social Work at the University of Missouri–Columbia, and Joseph is in private practice in Columbia, MO. In "Community-

Responsive Partners for Environmental Health," Lorette Picciano, director of Rural Coalition in Washington, DC, continues the health care theme as she describes several coalitions, outlines professional skills that social workers need in rural areas, and advocates for professional and community partnerships. Finally, Dwight Williams's comments on Picciano's article add additional insight to the issues presented.

In Part 3, collaborations, partnerships, and the strengths perspective are described by Ann Weick, dean of the School of Social Welfare at the University of Kansas; Patricia McDonald, graduate student in social welfare at SUNYA; Katsi Cook, School of Public Health, SUNYA; Katharine Briar-Lawson, head of the social work doctoral program at the University at Utah, and Hal Lawson, professor, University of Utah; and Kathleen O'Brien, principal of East Greenbush Central School in Albany. A response to McDonald's article by Gloria Reynolds, graduate public health student at SUNYA, is also included in this section.

The conclusion, "A Look toward the Future: Lessons Learned" by Joan Levy Zlotnik, summarizes the process used to generate and discuss the themes and concepts related to collaborative preparation of helping professionals for the community. Highlights from the focus group meeting and the papers presented, as well as recommendations for the future, are outlined in this section of the book.

Purpose of the Book

In theory, collaboration and coordination involve a fluid process through which diverse individuals or organizations undertake a joint initiative, solve a common problem, or work toward shared goals (Abramson & Rosenthal, 1995). But collaboration and coordination are not new concepts or activities for helping professionals such as social workers. Their work in hospitals, schools, and settlement houses has long required coordination and collaboration with other disciplines and professions to ensure effective client services (Abramson & Rosenthal, 1995). In recent years, government policies and programs have exerted greater influence over the purposes and goals of these relationships. The Carter administration encouraged private- and public-sector partnerships to produce more housing and economic opportunities. The 1988 Job Training Partnership Act (JTPA) signed by President Reagan continued the encouragement and was acclaimed for its mandated public and private partnerships targeted to ensure development of a better-qualified labor force. Both initiatives set the stage for today's emphasis on collaboration and coordination that is economically, rather than socially, focused.

Nearly 10 years after JTPA, partnerships involving community members, both private and public, continue. The purpose of this book is to draw into greater relief some of the goals and problems that define collaborative partnerships in the next century. The focus on rural communities inscribes these problems in a specific context, but the case study is meant to reflect beyond itself, as well. The collected chapters explore the ingredients necessary for effective collaboration and coordination among community members, and they assess the roles and responsibilities of helping professionals in the future.

In addition to the student-sponsored workshop mentioned previously, two other focus group meetings influenced the issues developed here. These focus groups, held in November 1989 at the Nelson A. Rockefeller Institute for Government in Albany, NY, and in February 1990 at Mississippi State University in Stoneville, MS, were organized around the topic "Linking the Private and Public Sectors to Support Rural Families and their Communities." From these many resources, the strengths, generalist, and systems perspectives emerged as central themes for the book. The importance of participatory democracy also arose, for the inclusion of so many participants with a diversity of interests, knowledge, skills, and cultural experiences was a highlight of the 1996 focus group. Students, community leaders, urban and rural residents, representatives from private- and public-sector institutions, and professional and academic administrators, staff, and faculty all participated in discussions.

All involved hope this book will provide a framework to assess and analyze the integration of practice and policy, address technological advances and their impacts on helping professions, encourage urban and rural coalitions, and identify "best practice" models for the future. The production of this book shows the benefits of a collaborative and coordinated effort.

Co-Sponsors of the Focus Group Meeting

Shirley J. Jones, Jo Ann Weatherwax, Carol Young, and Joan Levy Zlotnik served as co-sponsors of the focus group meeting. Because each worked on collaboration and professional development when asked to take part in this project, they entered the partnership with similar values and perspectives. For example, each of them viewed professional development as an ongoing process, saw information as a form of empowerment, and referred to the strengths, generalist, and systems perspectives to direct their assessments. In addition, each of the co-sponsors had an affiliation with a university.

Shirley J. Jones is a Distinguished Service Professor at the School of Social Welfare, SUNYA. She served as dean of the Graduate School of Social Work at the University of Southern Mississippi from 1977 to 1989. Her research focuses on rural families and their communities and rural community economic development. Jones served on the National Advisory Board of Rural Health from 1987 to 1991. She was the overall facilitator for this project.

Jo Ann Weatherwax played a major role in getting private sector participation at the focus group meeting. Weatherwax is director of the Institute for the Advancement of Health Care Management at the School of Business, SUNYA. She works on telecommunications in rural areas and offers courses on rural health management in the School of Business.

Carol D. Young is director of professional development and continuing education at the School of Public Health, SUNYA. As a cosponsor of the project, she worked with David Carpenter, dean of the School of Public Health, to provide community-based representation at the focus group meeting. Interactive television is part of her expertise.

Joan Levy Zlotnik took time from a busy schedule to help cosponsor the focus group meeting. Zlotnik is the director of special projects for CSWE. The Ford Foundation, the National Institute of Mental Health, and the W.K. Kellogg Foundation have funded her research on interdisciplinary collaboration and partnerships. She is an adjunct professor at the University of Maryland School of Social Work, where she is completing her doctoral studies in public child welfare. Zlotnik secured a W.K. Kellogg grant for the funding of this publication.

Students from SUNYA's School of Social Welfare, School of Public Health, School of Education, and School of Business also contributed to the planning of the focus group meeting. Students presenting at the meeting were selected from a group responding to a call for papers. Graduate student Patricia McDonald (School of Social Welfare) and recent doctoral graduate Kathleen A. O'Brien (School of Education) were keynote speakers at the focus group meeting. Student discussants included graduate students Gloria Reynolds (School of Public Health) and Marissa Panton and James Izzo (School of Business). Five graduate students from the School of Social Welfare collaborated on an article for this publication: Irene Cody, Kristine Collins, `Linda Mokarry, Mark Morris, and Kim Rosekrans. School of Social Welfare graduate students Dawn Knight Thomas and Barbara Roginski served as focus group volunteers, and recent social welfare graduate Steve Siegard served as official recorder.

Most of the participants at the focus group meeting were members of the social work, public health, education, and business professions. The meeting planners inevitably looked to their respective profession for experts willing to underwrite portions of their own travel and lodging. Because social work was cited in most of the papers presented at this meeting, it will be the model most referred to in this book. The co-editors are aware that there are other helping professions, each with its own goals and mission, and they hope that the use of social work as a model will be understood and its strengths applied.

References

Abramson, J., & Rosenthal, B. (1995). Interdisciplinary and inter-organizational collaboration. In R. L. Edwards (Ed.-in-Chief), *Encyclopedia of social work* (19th ed., pp. 1479-1489). Washington, DC: NASW Press.

Brueggemann, W. G. (1996). The practice of macro social work. Chicago: Nelson-Hall.

Jones, S. J. (1996). *Collaboration and coordination regarding rural social work and economic development.* Unpublished manuscript, State University of New York at Albany.

Kahn, A. J. (1969). *Theory and practice of social planning.* New York: Russell Sage Foundation.

Netting, F. E., Kettner, T., & McMurtry, S. (1993). *Social work macro practice.* White Plains, NY: Longman.

Acknowledgments

The W.K. Kellogg Foundation, with the help of Program Director Gloria T. Meert, provided a grant to CSWE to publish this book. Dean Lynn Videka-Sherman of the School of Social Welfare, SUNYA, and Dean David Carpenter of the School of Public Health, SUNYA, offered moral as well as financial support. The School of Business and the University Auxiliary Services (UAS) at SUNYA helped defray the cost of facilities and meals for the focus group meeting. Through the support of Donald Beless and Joan Levy Zlotnik, CSWE made financial contributions to ensure the success of the overall project.

The participants who evaluated the focus group meeting (*N*=19) rated it very highly. Two major comments expressed by the respondents were: "the interdisciplinary communication and commitment shown at this meeting helped to make it a success," and there is a "need to continue and extend the collaboration established at this meeting." The co-editors agree this project has been dynamic in nature and thank Carol D. Young for capturing its spirit in her paper entitled "Making Stone Soup: Collaboration and Cooperation," which will serve as a prologue to the ensuing section. We extend thanks to all who helped make this book a reality.

Making Stone Soup: Collaboration and Cooperation

Carol D. Young

> *In the folk tale, a hungry and clever soldier promises to make delicious soup from a stone. All he asks of each villager is to add an ingredient to the pot.*

This meeting was a delicious and satisfying stone soup. Gathering ingredients was as much a collaboration as putting them together. Shirley J. Jones provided the stone—her version of an event that would honor student papers, bring together experts from across campus and across the country, and include good discussion and good thinking in an intimate, elegant setting. She secured a small grant from the University at Albany and went in search of co-sponsors to add more to the pot. In theory, each co-sponsor would match the seed money and invite two presenters, two discussants, and six participants. In reality, each co-sponsor brought whatever funding they could muster (some cash, mostly travel, and mostly in-kind support). The most delicious ingredients came from our professional networks: the presenters, discussants, and participants involved.

We did not know exactly what to expect or how our soup would taste—a mixture of three professional schools, a national council, the Kellogg Foundation, a medical school, students, professors, a midwife, a community organizer, public health directors, a county social service commissioner, and more. Would the mixture be incompatible, undercooked, indigestible? No, we trusted each other and the soup took on a life of its own. Several strong, unifying flavors emerged in the recipe for this soup: have a leader with a vision, listen to and respect all the partners, rely on trust rather than control, develop more in a circular than a linear mode.

And the proof was in the eating. Enthusiastic reviews asked for more ingredients—greater community representation and more mixing and intermingling of the ingredients—and more chance to talk.

Part 1

FRAMING THE AGENDA

Although many current social and economic problems will continue into the next century, rapid social and technological changes will undoubtedly bring unprecedented problems. Helping professionals will need special practice competencies to carry out their roles and responsibilities for the 21st century, and institutions that train future practitioners must work to anticipate changes.

Shirley J. Jones advocates this proactive stance in Chapter 1, "Professional Development in the Human Services: Implications for the 21st Century," asserting that social workers and other helping professionals should take leadership roles in education and society. She asserts that professional development will have to foster critical thinking and technical competence in resources such as computers and interactive television. Familiar subjects like collaboration and coordination, technology, and economic and social development will be revisited for new missions and goals that will affect professional education and training. She also suggests innovative partnerships involving urban and rural collaboration and coordination between groups at national and international levels.

Joan Levy Zlotnik continues the focus on the roles and responsibilities of helping professionals by focusing on community needs and supports. She cites more integrated public service programs as one way to support community residents, and collaboration as a way to create a comprehensive service system. Zlotnik describes examples of "best practice" public partnerships and lists some of the characteristics of effective partnerships, referring also to some problems and limitations in developing them. Using the strengths perspective, she encourages university–community partnerships, because their structure offers interdisciplinary support and expertise in bringing about effective change.

The final chapter in Part 1 is an example of the positive outcomes of collaboration and partnership. Written by five graduate students, "Social Workers Facing the 21st Century: Are We Ready?" provided the authors opportunities to talk with their peers from other disciplines about the world in which they will practice during the next century. The authors express concern that they are being shortchanged by the educational emphasis on specialization in social work. They recommend that social work education produce practitioners who are competent and effective in transferring their skills to a variety of agencies and geographic areas. The generalist approach provides a model for the 21st century practitioner, they assert, adding that one implication of this emphasis is that the amount of time spent in degree completion would have to be broadened.

1

Professional Development in the Human Services: Implications for the 21st Century

Shirley J. Jones

While social workers and other human service practitioners continually face problems caused by prevailing economic and political conditions, for the most part they have not been properly trained to address the conditions themselves. Rapid changes in today's information age, combined with students' desire to complete their education at a reasonable cost, make it increasingly difficult for social work educators to address such problems in their curricula. This chapter explores issues and problems related to the professional development of social workers. It explores potential roles and functions for the 21st century and offers recommendations for the education and training required to better support clients and client systems.

As we move into the next century, social workers and social work educators must continue to ask about the place of social work and other helping professions in society. In his book *Megatrends 2000*, John Naisbitt (1990) asserts that the most exciting question of the 21st century will not pertain to technology, but to what it means to be human. He places social work and other helping professions at the forefront in determining the answer to this question, but we must ask: Is social work aware of its future roles? And what knowledge, skills, and values will social workers need to carry out these roles?

To begin to answer these questions about the role of professional development as a means for change, the author has undertaken a review of the social work literature, conducted studies on rural social work and community-wide economic development, and gathered focus group findings on support to rural families and their communities. A generalist perspective informs the discussion, and rural social work offers a lens for examining some of its issues and problems. Together, generalist theory and rural social work begin to address the problem of empowering practitioners to respond to client problems and their causes.

Responsibilities Past and Future

Social work has long worked on problems of poverty, oppression, industrialization, and urbanization (Hartman, 1990). Unfortunately, these problems will not diminish in the 21st century, but only grow in scope. Funds for social programs and resources for social services will continue to be scarce, and categorical grants will encourage competition among agencies to secure these limited resources. Federal government requirements that communities take primary responsibility for their self-sufficiency will result in local governments stressing economic development over social development. In addition, welfare reform and downsizing at social agencies will require the virtual reinvention of the human services.[1]

As more social workers concentrate efforts to advocate for community needs and services, they will need to adapt to new conditions. Growing diversity in populations will require social workers to better understand multiculturalism, racism, inequality, and inequity. A technology and information society will expect social workers to be computer literate and able to gain access to resources through many channels. The growing emphasis on managed care, cost-effectiveness, and competition for limited funds will increase the need for social workers to facilitate partnerships with other disciplines (e.g., public health, education, and business) and with the grassroots community. An increase in self-help groups will encourage social work to develop as a viable model for all helping professions and to become more proactive in strategies to compete effectively and responsibly in the marketplace (Hopps & Collins, 1995; Johnson, 1989).

The future dictates a leadership role for helping professionals working with local and regional populations, participating in national and international partnerships, and facilitating teamwork among a diverse group of people. Social workers in the 21st century will have to continue to think critically; master the use of computers

---

[1] These issues formed the topics of discussion in the following focus group meetings: "Linking the Public and Private Sectors to Support Rural Families," November 1989, held at the Nelson A. Rockefeller Institute for Government, Albany, NY; a follow-up to that meeting, February 1990, sponsored by Mississippi State University, Stoneville, MS; and "Professional Development of Helping Professions in Rural Communities," October/November 1996, held at the Nelson A. Rockefeller Institute for Government, Albany, NY.

and other technology; understand how economic development interfaces with community development; appreciate differences; deal with pressure; remain committed to the call of service; and willingly advocate for social justice and equality (Hopps & Collins, 1995).

Using a strengths perspective (Weick, Rapp, Sullivan, & Kisthardt, 1989), social workers can think of these problems and barriers as windows of opportunity. The goal of a strengths perspective is to move away from a pathological model to a goal-focused model centered on a client's perception of where to go with her or his life. This perspective can be translated to a macro level, where social workers have monitored and evaluated policy issues affecting families and their communities, including the welfare reform–driven Personal Responsibility and Work Opportunity Reconciliation Act of 1996. Social workers can inform and educate legislators and the general public about the needs of welfare recipients, such as child care and transportation; they can identify legislative components that will better empower recipients, such as education and training; and they can advocate for changes or modifications in laws and programs, as in the case of workfare and community service participation.

Planned change is not an easy task, for the change process is often disjointed and incremental and its outcome not realized immediately (Kettner, Daley, & Nichols, 1985). Most social workers resist planning for change on a macro level, because they lack concrete knowledge and skills to work with large systems like communities, organizations, and social groups (McInnis-Dittrich, 1994). Many direct practice social work students express feeling overwhelmed by macro practice courses, with many only taking these courses when they are mandated. Somehow, social work education has not made macro courses exciting, relevant, or both for students—a concern that extends to field practice, too, which has problems bridging the gap between micro and macro.

Macro skills will grow in relevance in coming decades, and schools of social work will need to better market macro-level knowledge and skills to train social workers for the future. One suggestion is to include more experiential and hands-on activities in the curriculum. Student learning would be directed at critical thinking and developing strategic plans and actions. Student and faculty partnerships, for example, could consist of working together on advocacy projects, writing grants, and presenting conference papers. These types of experiences produce important educational outcomes, such as better appreciation of human strengths and of the relationship between micro and macro practice.

Collaboration in Education and Practice

To produce effective planned change, social workers must examine opportunities for collaboration and coordination. Social workers have historically served in settings that require them to establish partnerships with other disciplines and service agencies (Abramson & Rosenthal, 1995). However, increased incentives for collaborative work have emerged over the last two decades, premised more on economic efficiency than on other social reasons. The many public and private partnerships developed in recent years have provided definite social outcomes, and business and government continue to encourage partnerships to develop a more qualified labor force, create more jobs, and encourage community self-sufficiency.

Examples of this abound. During the Carter administration, an emphasis on public and private partnerships in housing resulted in more housing units built in poor and oppressed communities and more job opportunities for residents. In 1988, President Reagan signed into law the Job Training Partnership Act (JTPA), which mandated public and private partnerships to ensure employment opportunities and training. And so far, the 1990s' era of retrenchment, downsizing, and reform has brought an increase in partnerships to help agencies and local governments coordinate scarce financial and staff resources and an increase in collaboration among advocacy groups to lobby legislators at all levels of government.

Collaboration and coordination during the 21st century will have global reaches, as communities and their residents are affected more directly by global issues. Burgeoning networks will respond to concerns such as AIDS, women's rights and protection, terrorism, and the effects of growing competitive markets on communities, especially in rural areas. These problems suggest multifaceted approaches that require social workers to practice in new arenas at regional, national, and international levels. Social work educators must thus be prepared to teach students more about the forces, characteristics, goals, and outcomes of collaboration and coordination in a global information society.

Some of the forces that foster collaboration include *mandating partnerships*, such as those created by JTPA; developing *professional networks* across disciplines; using *visionary leadership, common vision,* and *crisis* to encourage novel partnerships; and creating *broker-type partnerships* to address short-term issues and problems (Waddock, 1988). To generate successful coalitions, social workers must understand leading concepts such as mutual benefits, interdependence, reciprocity, concerted action, and joint production (Abramson & Rosenthal, 1995). Professional training must provide social workers with this knowledge, and practitioners must, in turn, be willing and able to impart such knowledge and skills to their client systems.

Even though social workers are familiar with economic concepts such as supply, demand, markets, and profits, many are educated from a social perspective and do not think of intervention strategies in economic terms (Chambers, 1995). Direct-service or micro-practice social workers, for example, face cost and funding issues less often than indirect-service or macro practitioners (Gilbert & Specht, 1986). The present national and global focus on economic concerns demands that helping professionals become more aware of economic perspectives on planning, policy, and programming. The general public's need to place the brunt of the nation's economic problems on social service programs requires that helping professionals understand the brutal, if contradictory, fact that social spending is minuscule in some areas. They must better understand the fiscal implications of federal decentralization of social spending and how states and local governments decide how to use funds to implement social programs. Finally, social workers and other helping professionals must understand the impact of global economics on urban and rural communities (Gilbert & Specht, 1986; Haynes & Mickelson, 1991).

The need for change has also affected the field of economics. In *The Future of Capitalism*, Thurow (1996) describes how economic ideologies will be redefined by economic changes touched off by events such as the end of communism, the rise of the information age, a growing world population, and the absence of a dominant economic, political, or military power. With opportunities like this, social workers, in collaboration with communities and other helping professionals, can join in economic debates about market systems that promote well-being for all people. Such partnerships, however, are predicated on schools of social work building courses into their curriculum that help students better understand market systems, the political and economic framework of planning, policy, and programming, and the relationship between social and economic development. As Christenson, Fendley, and Robinson (1989) state, development "is concerned historically with the transition of cultures, countries, and communities from less advanced to more advanced social stages" (p. 9). Development focuses on economic prosperity and, they add, "includes the institutional transformation of structures to facilitate technological advancement and improve-

ment in the production and distribution of goods and services."
Course content on development can thus illustrate the socioeconomic nexus for students and can increase students' competencies
for collaborative work in the future.

In addition, students should learn management, negotiating,
leadership, and advocacy skills that enable them to facilitate and
participate in the process of shaping economic and political ideologies. Social workers in community-based organizations must be
prepared to help these agencies use microeconomic activities for
community empowerment, and they must be able to provide social
support for economic development efforts such as enterprise
zones. Family and organizational fiscal management workshops are
just a few of the activities that can be designed through student,
faculty, and community partnerships to benefit all involved.

The tie between community development and individual well-
being remains a prime focus for social workers, and its economic
side cannot be neglected. Though community development (CD)
has many definitions, its primary goal is to help people improve
their social and economic situation, rather than react to it. To this
end, according to Christenson, Fendley, and Robinson (1989), CD
follows a three-part approach similar to Rothman's (1986) three
models of community organization (CO). The CD approaches are
self-help, technical assistance, and conflict, while CO focuses on
locality development, social planning, and social action. Bonnett
(1993) also notes that economic development is primarily directed
to job creation, and most local governments influenced by federal-
ism are setting priorities based on this goal. Christenson, Fendley,
and Robinson (1989) indicate that economic development is chiefly
concerned with increasing productivity and efficiency to improve
the economic situation of a locality. But economic development
cannot be effectively achieved without healthy, educated, and
contented people.

Shaffer and Summers (1989) recognize a tension between
advocates whose primary intervention goal is to achieve development *in* the community and those who want development *of* the
community. Development *of* the community concerns the quality of
the relationships among residents of a locality and integrates key
factors such as cohesive and integrative structures. Development *in*
the community treats the community as a locality in which social,
political, and economic activities occur regularly and through
different organizational formats. In this sense, the community is
treated as if it were a business, where the goal is to create appropriate jobs and raise the real income of the community itself. An

effective social worker should thus be able to link both approaches to ensure a community economic development model that benefits the entire locality. For Christenson, Fendley, and Robinson (1989), this involves creating and regenerating accessible institutions that empower and improve the well-being of residents. For future social workers, it implies an ability to be flexible in their interventions, whether it be with local businesses and organizations or with residents themselves.

Such joint partnerships are necessary now more than ever given the changing global economy, and rural America can be used as a case study for preparing helping professionals. Over the past two decades companies and factories have left rural areas and located overseas in order to secure inexpensive labor (Bonnett, 1993). This has resulted in shop closures, high unemployment rates, out-migration, increased poverty among women and children, and increased numbers of mental health cascs due to stress and depression. Joint efforts by schools of social work and rural communities have already begun to address this global impact. A university–community collaboration illustrates this point.

In spring 1997, two classes at the School of Social Welfare, State University of New York, University at Albany, worked with their professor to support rural families and their communities. One class in macro social work held a workshop to educate the general public about the needs of rural communities. The other rural social work class collected data on the needs of a particular rural legislative district in relation to welfare reform; during the state's social work lobby day, the class met with the state legislator's office and advocated on behalf of rural welfare recipients. This university–community partnership benefits all involved. First, for students and the professor, it provides a service and learning component with hands-on practical experience and a community laboratory to test theoretical concepts. Students especially gain a sense of empowerment from utilizing their knowledge to benefit communities. Second, it bridges the gap between the university and the community by engaging in a community-centered, educationally focused enterprise designed to achieve sustained improvement in social services. Finally, it elevates the stature of the social work profession among state legislators, the university's administration, and the grassroots community.

Rural communities have historically survived on the collaborative efforts of neighbors and relatives who formed partnerships and used social networks to help with farming chores, home building, and child care (Ginsberg, 1993; Martinez-Brawley, 1980). But recent economic problems affecting individuals, groups, families, and communities have eroded traditional rural partnerships and social networks. Out-migration due to high unemployment rates, farmers seeking employment off the farms to support their families, a federal system requiring state and local governments to become more self-sufficient, and increasing numbers of people needing mental health services because of depression and stress due to unemployment and poverty (Jones, 1993) have diminished the traditional mechanisms of participation and support. This suggests that new partnerships and social networks have to be invented.

Social workers and other helping professionals will have to develop closer partnerships with rural families and their communities to assist in securing limited funds, resources, and technical assistance. They must recognize an urban bias that has resulted in federal and state government attention to solutions to economic and social problems (Hewitt, 1993). This bias has also influenced the inequities between urban and rural salary ranges and other supports and services, including salaries in social work, which are generally lower in rural areas (Ginsberg, 1993).

Statistics show that while national and international economic changes affect urban and rural areas alike, many rural communities have been hit harder than their urban counterparts (Jones, 1989; Porter, 1989). Rural America also has unique concerns. Most rural communities do not have accessible and affordable transportation, housing, and social services (Jones, 1993). In addition to shrinking public services, rural America has faced unique social and economic transitions for the last few decades. This is illustrated by the loss of small family farms to large corporations and by the loss of approximately 94% of the land owned by black farmers since 1920. Mining and other natural-base industries have also been replaced by manufacturing and service industries. In response, legislators have shown a growing interest in building jails in rural areas to create more jobs and revenue. This change has not resulted in higher salaries, however, but in high unemployment, out-migration, and increased poverty rates (Jones, 1993, 1994).[2]

The comparative lack of health care and human service workers in rural areas in turn affects rural economic development. Most local governments do not have the technical assistance and staff to compete for federal and state grants, which means that fewer rural communities are included in programs such as economic enterprise zone programs.[3] These economic deficits have exacerbated mental health stresses on many rural individuals and families, though few accessible and affordable services are available to help people address these problems.

Although the plight of rural America suggests that more social workers are needed in rural communities, schools of social work are not promoting or preparing students to become rural social workers. Even programs located in rural states are not addressing rural issues, including New York. Approximately two thirds of New York's counties are classified as rural. However, none of the schools of social work in the state have a rural subspecialization. In response, at the State University of New York, University at Albany (SUNYA), the School of Social Welfare has developed an advanced policy course on rural social work, the Institute of Health Care Management in the School of Business is developing a course on rural health care management, and the School of Public Health has appointed a rural health policy specialist to its faculty.

Social work is not the only discipline not promoting or preparing students to work in rural communities. Deleon, Wakefield, and Vanden-Bos (1993) note shortages of health personnel in other disciplines, including psychology and medicine, throughout rural America. Proposals for federal- and state-funded scholarships and the development of "home grown" personnel have been offered to encourage recruitment and retention of rural human service workers. The potential for funding and implementing these ideas, however, is dampened by the nation's present economic and political climate.

Economic changes continue to influence migration from rural to urban areas, and in states such as New York where people can easily travel between urban and rural areas in a short time, new concerns arise. Small towns and rural areas of New York are witnessing more drug trafficking and related crimes; police reports indicate that much of the drugs and criminals are coming from New

[2] These issues were also at the forefront of the discussion in the student-sponsored "Workshop on Rural Social Work and Economic Development in the 21st Century," held at SUNYA in April 1996.

[3] For example, New York State's Economic Development Zones (EDZ) program was created in 1986 to stimulate growth in economically distressed communities, and revised tax incentives in 1993 sought further to boost business and employment growth in selected areas of the state, with special financial incentives and technical assistance for new and expanding businesses, including loans, job training, wage-tax credits, sales-tax rebates, utility rate reductions, and zone-based corporate tax credits. The federal government presently funds enterprise zones and "champion programs" through the Department of Housing and Urban Development, while the Department of Agriculture sponsors rural EDZ programs.

York City and other large cities (New York State Office of Rural Affairs, 1990). Statistics also show an increase in the number of AIDS victims returning to rural areas to be with their families and formerly homeless persons living in crowded homes of relatives. Lack of statistical data about rural problems make it difficult to assess the needs of rural communities, and as a result neglected rural areas face a form of silent suffering. Research about relationships between urban and rural areas suggests that social workers and other helping professionals can serve as facilitators to foster urban and rural collaboration and coordination (Jones, 1994; Martinez-Brawley, 1990). Preparation for this role requires the knowledge and skills to design and implement needs assessments and other research tools; it will also demand training in cultural diversity.

To begin to redress these issues, a focus group meeting held October 31 and November 1, 1996, brought together a diverse group whose interests centered on professional development of social workers and other practitioners. Representatives from social work, health, business, and education were gathered, making a group that included faculty members, administrators, students, community-based workers, and foundation staff from urban and rural areas. Discussions at this gathering reinforced the need for more interdisciplinary partnerships to facilitate community change. The group discussed barriers that discourage these types of interdisciplinary partnerships, especially technical terminology, values, lack of encouragement by universities, competition for limited funds, and student enrollment. The response at SUNYA has been to identify professors addressing rural issues and to establish a group to explore and assess potential student, faculty, and community partnerships to promote economic development for all people, particularly those in oppressed and poor communities.

Summary

Unless schools of social work and other professional schools are willing to prepare their students to address 21st-century problems, future practitioners will become irrelevant to communities. To prevent this, educators must begin to develop effective educational and professional paradigms for the future. A list of questions developed from the focus group meeting is provided in closing. It is hoped that this list will motivate you to add additional questions, continue the discussion on an interdisciplinary level, and take action regarding the preparation needed for helping professionals for the 21st century.

1. Will the social worker of the future be a generalist or specialist?

2. Will the generalist approach adequately equip social workers of the future?

3. What knowledge and skills should be highlighted for future social workers?

4. How will collaboration, coordination, and partnership activities differ in the 21st century, and what are the implications for social work education and training?

5. How do social work educators build economic concepts into the curriculum in a nonthreatening manner?

6. What technology should be introduced to social work students to better equip them to work with individuals, groups, families, and communities?

References

Abramson, J., & Rosenthal, B. (1995). *Interdisciplinary and inter-organizational collaboration.* Washington, DC: NASW Press.

Bonnett, T. (1993). *Strategies for rural competitiveness: Policy options for state governments.* Washington, DC: Council of Governor's Policy Advisors.

Chambers, D. (1995). Economic analysis. In R. L. Edwards (Ed.-in-Chief), *Encyclopedia of social work* (19th ed., p. 824). Washington, DC: NASW Press.

Christenson, J., Fendley, K. & Robinson, J., Jr. (1989). Community development. In J. Christenson & J. Robinson, Jr. (Eds.), *Community development in perspective* (pp. 3-25). Ames: Iowa State University Press.

Deleon, P., Wakefield, M., & Vanden-Bos, G. (1993). Health care in rural America: A national priority. In S. J. Jones (Ed.), *Sociocultural and service issues in working with rural clients* (pp. 77-91). Albany, NY: Rockefeller College Press.

Gilbert, N., & Specht, H. (1986). *Dimensions of social welfare policy.* Englewood Cliffs, NJ: Prentice-Hall.

Ginsberg, L. (1993). *Social work in rural communities.* Alexandria, VA: Council on Social Work Education.

Hartman, A. (1990). Education for direct practice. *Families in Society: The Journal of Contemporary Human Services, 71*(2), 44-50.

Haynes, S., & Mickelson, J. (1991). *Affecting change: Social workers in the political arena.* New York: Longman.

Hewitt, M. (1993). Defining "rural" areas: Impact on health care policy and research. In S. J. Jones (Ed.), *Sociocultural and service issues working with rural clients* (pp. 9-32). Albany, NY: Rockefeller College Press.

Hopps, J., & Collins, P. (1995). Social work profession overview. In R. L. Edwards (Ed.-in-Chief), *Encyclopedia of social work* (19th ed., pp. 2266-2282). Washington, DC: NASW Press.

Johnson, L. (1989). *Social work practice: A generalist approach.* Boston: Allyn and Bacon.

Jones, S. J. (1989, November). *Linking the public and private sectors to support rural families.* Paper presented at the Focus Group Meeting, Nelson A. Rockefeller Institute for Government, Albany, NY.

Jones, S. J. (Ed.). (1993). *Sociocultural and service issues working with rural clients.* Albany, NY: Rockefeller College Press.

Jones, S. J. (1994). Silent suffering: The plight of rural Black America. In B. Tidwell (Ed.), *State of Black America* (pp. 171-188). New York: National Urban League.

Kettner, P., Daley, J., & Nichols, A. (1985). *Initiating change in organizations and communities.* Monterey, CA: Brooks/Cole.

Martinez-Brawley, E. (1980). *Rural social welfare.* University Park, PA: Pennsylvania State University Press.

McInnis-Dittrich, K. (1994). *Integrating social welfare policy and social work practice.* Pacific Grove, CA: Brooks/Cole.

Naisbitt, J. (1990). *Megatrends 2000.* New York: Warner.

New York State Office of Rural Affairs. (1990, June). *Statistical profile of rural New York.* Albany: Author.

Porter, K. H. (1989). *Poverty in rural America: A national overview.* Washington, DC: Center on Budget and Policy Priorities.

Shaffer, R., & Summers, G. F. (1989). Community economic development. In J. Christenson and J. Robinson (Eds.), *Community organization in perspective* (pp. 173-195). Ames: Iowa State University Press.

Thurow, L. C. (1996). *The future of capitalism.* New York: William Morrow.

Waddock, S. A. (1988, Summer). Building successful social partnerships. *Sloan Management Review.* Cambridge, MA: Industrial Management Review Association, Alfred P. Sloan School of Management, Massachusetts Institute of Technology.

Weick, A., Rapp, C., Sullivan, P., & Kisthardt, W. (1989). The strengths perspective for social work practice. *Social Work, 34,* 350-354.

Selected Bibliography

Anderson, D., & Dawes, S. (1993). Information entrepreneurs: The missing link in providing services to rural families at risk. In S. J. Jones (Ed.), *Sociocultural and service issues in working with rural clients.* Albany, NY: Rockefeller College Press.

Cornelia F., & Christenson, J. (1991). *Rural policies for the 1990s.* Boulder, CO: Westview.

Eberts, P. (1994). *Socioeconomic trends in New York state: 1950–1990.* Albany: New York State Legislative Commission on Rural Resources.

Harris, N. (1995). *Social work education and public human services partnerships.* Alexandria, VA: Council on Social Work Education.

Heffernan, J. W. (1992). *Social welfare policy.* White Plains, NY: Longman.

Jansson, B. (1990). *Social welfare policy from theory to practice.* Belmont, CA: Wadsworth.

Martinez-Brawley, E. (1993). Allied health professionals and rural families: A natural collaboration. In S. J. Jones (Ed.), *Sociocultural and service issues in working with rural clients* (pp. 239-244). Albany, NY: Rockefeller College Press.

Martinez-Brawley, E. (1995). Knowledge diffusion and transfer of technology: Conceptual promises and concrete steps for human services innovators. *Social Work, 40,* 670-682.

Netting, E., Kettner, P., & McMurtry (1993). *Social work macro practice.* White Plains, NY: Longman.

Zlotnik, J. (1993). *Social work education and public human services—Developing partnerships.* Alexandria, VA: Council on Social Work Education.

2

Preparing Human Service Workers for the 21st Century: A Challenge to Professional Education

Joan Levy Zlotnik

As we look to the future, it is necessary to examine the context in which human service programs will be delivered and to envision the practice competencies that social workers, teachers, nurses, public health specialists, psychologists, public administrators, and others will need to provide competent and effective services to children and families. Professional education, too, must anticipate changing service delivery needs and seek ways to fulfill and influence them. This chapter provides an overview of new paradigms for human service delivery; identifies the values, knowledge, and skills that future administrators, supervisors, and frontline practitioners will need; and examines strategies for university-based professional education programs that prepare practitioners for new roles.

New Paradigms for Service Delivery

Communities are contending with shrinking human service resources and greater opportunities to decide how to allocate them. Rising rates of poverty reflect a growing number of children, families, and older persons with increasingly complex social support needs related to health, economic security, housing, mental health, and education. Rural communities that historically have struggled with isolation, a scarcity of financial and social resources, and difficulties attracting competent professionals experience acute forms of these problems (Davenport & Davenport, 1995), and efforts to ease them can prove useful to other communities.

"Neighbor helping neighbor" efforts have been heralded for improving educational outcomes for children, promoting economic development, rebuilding community institutions, and preventing and treating child abuse and neglect (McClellan, 1995; Melaville & Blank, 1993; U.S. Advisory Board on Child Abuse and Neglect, 1993). Recently, some communities have attempted to address socioeconomic problems through community-based initiatives that build on the community's strengths and link government and community agencies, corporations, religious organizations, and families to address community needs (Sorenson & Washington, 1994). Efforts to create integrated service delivery have brought together health, mental health, education, economic security, and social service programs. Service improvement efforts such as school-linked services, one-stop service centers, and family support centers require collaboration and partnerships among service providers and families and among agency administrators, funders, and policymakers. Kahn and Kamerman (1992) have described these as examples of "service integration," which they define as:

> a systematic effort to solve problems of service fragmentation and of the lack of an exact match between an individual and family with problems and needs and an interventive program or professional specialty. The effort may take the form of (a) high level or local-level administrative restructuring or collaboration, or (b) case-oriented strategies at the service delivery level. (p. 5)

These new service delivery paradigms are based on principles such as:

- Services should be family-centered, community-based, preventive, comprehensive, and flexible.
- Services should be defined in terms of the family's strengths and self-defined problems, goals, needs, and solutions.
- Service planning should include the family as a partner, and services should be tailored to fit families rather than force them to fit into categorical services.
- Problems and solutions should be defined in terms of the family's culture, ethnicity, and heritage.

These principles are adapted from "Family Support Principles" developed by the National Association of Social Workers (NASW) Commission on Families (1991) and are similar to ones articulated by many groups and organizations struggling to prevent and intervene effectively in economic, social, and health problems (Cole, 1995; McClellan, 1995).

In 1994, over 50 national organizations reached consensus on a separate set of principles for creating community-based and school-linked education, health, and human service systems for children, youth, and families (American Academy of Pediatrics, 1994). They stressed collaboration in creating a comprehensive service system and identified the need for public, private, and community services delivered in a coordinated, integrated, and collaborative way. They recommended a move from piecemeal service delivery to comprehensive service delivery, and emphasized that new roles for human service professionals will require effective collaboration with other disciplines and across programs.

One effort to develop more collaborative and comprehensive delivery of human services is the "Together We Can" project, a national leadership-building initiative that helps communities create collaboratives between public and private agencies, government, and community and neighborhood institutions and members. It grew from an initiative of the U.S. Department of Health and Human Services and the U.S. Department of Education to develop "a guide for crafting a pro-family system of education and human services" (Melaville & Blank, 1993, p. iii). The guide encourages a holistic approach to treating children and family problems, easy access to comprehensive services, early detection of problems, use of preventive health care services, and flexibility in the use of federal and state funds for education, health, and human services. The initiative also stresses hiring and preparing staff who are able to work in these new service delivery environments. Administrators, supervisors, policymakers, and frontline staff must incorporate the "family support principles" into their practice and have the necessary collaborative skills, knowledge, and ability to:

- Incorporate other co-workers' perspectives;
- Work with people from different systems;
- Communicate across organizational boundaries and with every part of the community;
- Build commitment to a shared vision;
- Creatively confront tough issues;
- Nurture leadership in others;
- Appreciate cultural differences; and
- Deal constructively with tension created by diversity (Melaville & Blank, 1993)

Linking delivery of public human services with families and other community-based resources is of particular concern in rural communities, where health, mental health, and social services are more likely to be delivered by public agencies than in larger communities (Davenport & Davenport, 1995). As agencies respond to demands for shifts in service delivery structure, they need to identify the knowledge, skills, and values that their future work force will require. In addition to the collaborative leadership skills identified by Melaville & Blank (1993), frontline workers need to:

- Emphasize client strengths, rather than client pathology, and use client strengths and resources in problem solving.
- View their clients holistically and develop service plans that encompass a broad range of factors.
- Join with clients as partners in a collaborative problem-solving effort.
- Tailor treatment plans to meet the needs and goals of clients.
- Work with clients to create specific, short-term measurable goals.
- Demonstrate skill in engaging clients in a trusting working relationship, expressing appropriate empathy, and fostering development of a broad range of life skills (Kinney, Strand, Hagerup, & Bruner, 1994).

Bricker-Jenkins (1992) emphasizes building strengths-oriented practice in public social services. Such practice should be constructed from the client's perspective of what works, beginning with an exploration of the client's basic needs. It should also relate to the client's strengths and resources, emphasizing, identifying, engaging, developing, and mobilizing ones that already exist in the client's life (p. 131). McCroskey (1996), too, underscores the relationship between worker and client in successful outcomes.

University–Community Partnerships

To take new roles in community development, health, education, and social service delivery, current human service professionals need training. To prepare future professionals for these roles, universities also need to take an active role in teaching necessary skills, values, and theoretical orientations for practice. Professional education programs that are responsive to family and community needs must be connected to an existing service delivery system, and, just as community agencies need to create partnerships, this and other tasks require collaborative ventures between universities and agencies.

Over the past several years, social work agencies and social work education programs have attempted to strengthen collaboration and partnerships between social work degree programs and public human service agencies. The greatest concentration of these partnership efforts has been in child welfare, where agencies struggle to recruit competent staff and social work education works to maintain its historic connection to this practice area (Child Welfare League of America, 1982). Universities have expanded their efforts to provide state-of-the-art curricula, supervise public child welfare field placements, and undertake planning, research, and evaluation projects in partnership with local agencies. These university–agency partnerships were frequently precipitated by a crisis, such as a class action lawsuit or intensive media attention to problems in the child welfare system after a sensationalized child death. Harris (1996) has identified the usual sequence of events in developing such partnerships:

- A precipitating event creates initial interest in partnership development;
- Key leaders become involved in negotiations;
- Purpose and vision of partnership are articulated;
- Needed resources are identified;
- Specific tasks and timelines are delineated, issues are resolved, and resources are obtained;
- Partnership is implemented.

This sequence not only relates to university–agency partnerships, but to new service delivery partnerships within communities that result from a crisis. Not all partnerships progress so smoothly, either. The need for all parties to accept common goals often means one party agrees to give up resources or shares them with others. In addition, although midlevel and frontline staff might commit to working with others to make programs less fragmented, involving leadership can prove more difficult. In other situations, a change in leadership can mean the partnership comes apart because of new priorities and goals.

The "Social Work Education and Public Human Services: Developing Partnerships" project, funded by the Ford Foundation and based at the Council on Social Work Education, has worked for the past four years to document the steps necessary for effective partnerships and to provide technical assistance for human service agencies and social work education programs to work together more successfully. Project partners have also been working with the U.S. Children's Bureau, the National Association of Public Child Welfare Agencies, the Child Welfare League of America, the National Association of Social Workers, and others to identify and promote successful strategies for the preparation of competent child welfare workers. The resulting collaboratives require commitment from social work education to prepare workers to meet the needs of vulnerable and oppressed children and their families; they also require commitment from public agencies to ensure they have workers with the necessary skills and knowledge for public human service practice. In the initial year of the project, participants identified several characteristics of successful collaboration (Zlotnik, 1993):

• Trusting relationships;
• Long-term commitment;
• Committed leaders;
• Benefits for all collaborators;
• Common interests and objectives.

Barriers to successful collaboration include:

• Differing organizational values;
• Differing philosophies;
• Differing reward systems;
• Global academic purposes versus specific needs of agencies;
• Lack of institutional commitment for the long term.

These characteristics also apply to collaboration between agencies, collaboration among disciplines, and collaboration between frontline workers and clients.

To prepare new workers for community-based practice, social work education programs have made changes in curricula, developed family-focused competencies that provide a framework for academic and field education, developed closer ties to agencies, and invited agency staff to participate as adjunct faculty. Many of these school–agency partnerships are supported by Title IV–E federal training funds or Title IV–B Section 426 discretionary grants (Harris, 1996). These grants have provided stipends for students, funded efforts to revise curricula with greater emphasis on strengths-based, family-focused, collaborative practice in the public sector; given agency staff an opportunity to receive a master's degree in social work; and used university faculty to staff field units in social work agencies.

Several universities are also involved in distance education efforts to bring undergraduate and graduate social work education programs to rural areas. Because human service professionals in rural areas often perform diverse tasks, a generalist approach to practice is consistent with job expectations (Davenport & Davenport, 1995), and preparation can be done in concord with a strengths-based, family-focused, empowerment approach to social work education.

Although child welfare forms the large part of university–agency collaborations, social work education programs are also partnering with agencies working in maternal and child health, mental health, and school and community development services (Cohen, 1996; Searcy, 1995; Zlotnik, 1993).

Lawson and Hooper-Briar (1994), Corrigan and Udas (1994), McCroskey (1996), and Melaville and Blank (1993), among others, not only articulate the need for multilateral collaborations between universities, agencies, and even staff and families, but also advocate further training for human service professionals through interprofessional education. Interprofessional strategies prepare workers to be flexible, to work as a team, and to understand the values and framework of other professions. The growing emphasis on shared case management and community-based service delivery strategies (Melaville & Blank, 1993) will make interprofessional skills more important in coming decades. To respond, professional education programs need to balance imparting professional knowledge and identity with developing teamwork and interprofessional collaborative practice. Rural communities, in particular, require professionals to have multiple skills and an understanding of perspectives from many professions. Collaboration and partnership across disciplines in universities is another place where collaboration is needed to prepare workers for the future. Social work education programs such as those at the University of Southern California, East Carolina University, California State University–Long Beach, University of Washington, Washington University, and Fordham University are actively involved in interprofessional education efforts to prepare social workers and other human service professionals for new paradigms of service delivery.

Conclusion

As the 21st century looms before us, we are beginning to look at new ways of doing business and new linkages that need to exist. Collaboration and partnerships are themes woven throughout practice with clients, practice with different agencies, projects linking public and private sectors, and programs joining universities and community agencies. Professionals cannot be educated in isolation, but must be educated to understand their kindred professions and to see families as partners in the change process. A strengths-based orientation to practice is helpful in bringing about positive change, as is the ability to develop trusting relationships. As we look to the future, universities, agencies, families, and neighborhoods must work together to build on each other's strengths, celebrate diversity, and seek economic security that will last a lifetime.

References

American Academy of Pediatrics. (1994). *Integrating education, health and human services for children, youth and families: Systems that are community-based and school-linked.* Washington, DC: Author.

Bricker-Jenkins, M. (1992). Building a strengths model of practice in the public social services. In D. Saleebey (Ed.), *The strengths perspective in social work practice* (pp. 122-136). White Plains, NY: Longman.

Child Welfare League of America. (1982). *Child welfare as a field of social work practice* (2nd ed.). New York: Author.

Cohen, D. (1996, February 26). A working relationship. *Education Week, p. 29.*

Cole, E. (1995). Becoming family centered: Child welfare's challenge. *Families in Society, 76*(3), 163-172.

Commission on Families. (1991). *Family support principles.* Washington, DC: National Association of Social Workers.

Corrigan, D., & Udas, K. (1994, September). *Interprofessional development and integrated services programs.* Paper presented at U.S. Department of Education and American Educational Research Association conference on school-linked comprehensive services for children and families, Leesburg, VA.

Davenport, J. A., & Davenport, J. (1995). Rural social work overview. In R. L. Edwards (Ed.-in-Chief), *Encyclopedia of social work* (19th ed., pp. 2076-2085). Washington, DC: NASW Press.

Harris, N. (1996). *Social work education and public human services partnerships: A technical assistance document.* Alexandria, VA: Council on Social Work Education.

Kahn, A., & Kamerman, S. (1992). *Integrating services integration: An overview of initiatives, issues and possibilities.* New York: National Center for Children in Poverty.

Kinney, J., Strand, K., Hagerup, M., & Bruner, C. (1994). *Beyond the buzzwords: Key principles in effective frontline practice.* Falls Church, VA: National Center for Service Integration.

Lawson, H., & Hooper-Briar, K. (1994). *Expanding partnerships: Involving colleges and universities in interprofessional collaboration and services integration.* Oxford, OH: Danforth Foundation and the Institute for Educational Research at Miami University.

McClellan, N. (1995). Redesigning services using an assets approach. In W. J. O'Neill (Ed.), *Family: The first imperative* (pp. 195-214). Cleveland, OH: O'Neill Foundation.

McCroskey, J. (1996, April). *Child welfare, family functioning and family preservation: Can we find a better balance?* Sixth Annual Louis Rainer Makofsky Lecture on Child Welfare, University of Maryland–Baltimore County.

Melaville, A., & Blank, M. (1993). *Together we can.* Washington, DC: U.S. Government Printing Office.

Searcy, J. (1995). *Higher education curricula for integrated services providers: Private foundations, public and private colleges and universities.* Monmouth, OR: Western Oregon State College, Teaching Research Division.

Sorenson, P., & Washington, V. (1994). *Joining forces: Strengthening the circle of caring communities for children.* Battle Creek, MI: Kellogg Foundation.

U.S. Advisory Board on Child Abuse and Neglect. (1993). *Neighbors helping neighbors: A new national strategy for the protection of children.* Washington, DC: Author.

Zlotnik, J. (1993). *Social work education and public human services: Developing partnerships.* Alexandria, VA: Council on Social Work Education.

3

Social Workers Facing the 21st Century: Are We Ready?

Irene Cody, Kristine Collins, Linda Mokarry, Mark Morris, and Kim Rosekrans

Social workers have long been—and should continue to be—at the forefront of social issues such as alcoholism, drug abuse, AIDS, domestic violence, gerontology, health care, welfare, teenage pregnancy, and declining family values. As Hopps and Collins (1995) note, future social workers and other professionals will continue to address issues like these and will be challenged by new ones. In the 21st century, social work educators will have to prepare students to meet the needs of increasingly diverse populations in contemporary communities, and without proper training to work on a variety of fronts, social workers will not evolve and bring about planned change effectively.

This chapter examines these curriculum issues, makes a case for a better programming model, and discusses some implications of such programming for the profession. It is spurred by concerns about the future that social workers and other helping professionals face and by questions about current social work education, including: Is the current social work curriculum giving future practitioners general knowledge to assess and intervene in a wide array of issues? What can be done to prepare future social workers for the many roles they will be expected to fulfill?

To be prepared for future careers, social work students must receive an education that promotes a generalist approach in the classroom and in the field. A generalist program entails clinical, management, and policy curriculum content. It teaches students to intervene at every level with an approach guided by planned change and an emphasis on the problem-solving process. As Anne Fortune put it, a generalist practitioner is "someone who does everything and hopefully does some of it well" (Fortune, 1996).

The Current Curriculum

Presently, most graduate schools of social work require students to complete one year of generalist study and then specialize in clinical or management practice in their second year. Although this training prepares students to meet many of the needs of vulnerable populations, students, educators, and practitioners alike should still ask if more can be done. Ultimately, this two-track curriculum is a disservice to both students and clients. By being forced into this dichotomy, clinical students leave the program without a strong understanding of management skills, while management students lack clinical skills. Also a result of this duality, clinical and management students leave without a strong grounding in social policy and activism.

As Hopps and Collins (1995) suggest, many educators and researchers consider the clinical and management models mutually exclusive and not complementary, and many social work curricula reflect this belief. The move toward specialization has polarized the social work profession. New recruits often come into the profession with hopes of a career as a private practitioner, and the notion of the social worker as an agent of social change tends to get lost. Schools of social welfare bear the responsibility for this trend.

Hopps and Collins (1995) argue that specialization "has posed a threat to the profession because the variety of perspectives have created tension, conflict and fragmentation" (p. 2272). Social workers can feel this tension when working collaboratively among themselves or with other professions. Social workers can work well together if they embrace the same generalist perspective. And when social workers come from a generalist education, they interface with people from other professions—interaction that, according to Stull (1996), discourages a narrow interdisciplinary focus and encourages more cross-disciplinary relationships for people of all disciplines. Orten and Rich (1988) note that it is not uncommon for at least six different professionals to work with an abusive family. An interdisciplinary focus would improve cooperation among practitioners, reduce needless overlap, and focus services on the best interests of clients.

A Model for Change and Its Implications

Teaching a generalist approach can help to "unify the profession and consolidate its identity" (Hopps & Collins, 1995). Today's social problems demand that social workers have a comprehensive mastery of management, policy, and clinical skills, and schools of social work should integrate all three components. How can we as social workers expect our clients to advocate for themselves or become involved politically in the system if we do not have such knowledge or ability ourselves? In addition, how can we expect our clients to improve their communication skills if we are not extensively trained to use these skills on all levels?

Echoing others' criticisms that social work programs can better prepare students to work in a variety of settings (Bernard, 1995; Davenport & Davenport, 1984; Jones, 1996), particularly in rural areas, the authors propose that schools of social work provide an education that will produce social workers who can competently and effectively transfer their skills to a variety of agencies, roles, and geographical areas. This is a tremendous task, but such a program can and should be provided so that social workers can better serve their clients, agencies, communities, and other service delivery systems.

This is not to suggest that all problems and interventions can be generalized to all people in all areas. As Davenport and Davenport (1984) point out, locality-based differences in social behavior exist, but a generalist education provides students with strong clinical, management, and policy skills to use effectively in different settings. For example, with the present programming, a social worker with a clinical specialization is not well equipped to work on an organizational, community, or policy level. Students from a generalist program, however, would be better prepared to work on all of these levels.

A generalist approach does not exclude gaining knowledge about specific client populations, agencies, or areas. Rather, it exposes students to multiple possibilities. By exploring similarities and differences between populations, generalist students will feel comfortable in the many roles they are expected to perform.

While Bernard (1995) notes that specialized knowledge is required to address the constantly emerging needs of our society, she also points out a need for more autonomous practitioners with broad service perspectives. An educational program that promotes a generalist approach throughout graduate study would provide students with this broad service perspective. One year of generalist study and one year of specialization is not enough to equip future social workers, Bernard states, and the authors feel it might be necessary to extend the MSW program one more year. Presently, one can earn an MSW degree in two years of full-time classes and field work. Advanced standing students can finish the program in only one year. An enormous amount of information in a relatively short time frame is fed to students, many of whom may have difficulty retaining and using all of the knowledge squeezed into a one- or two-year program. As practitioners, they then lack essential skills to address many current problems appropriately. Extending the program to three years would allow students to take the many courses offered in clinical, management, and policy arenas and produce better practitioners for the 21st century.

A three-year generalist approach to graduate studies is just one part of producing competent, effective social workers. Continuing education is another integral part of this expansion. This opportunity provides social workers with the ability to branch out into other areas of study, such as economics, public health, or business. Schools should not be the only sources of education, either. Agencies need to provide in-service training to educate their workers and should encourage them to attend conferences and seminars related to the field. This additional knowledge can only strengthen social workers' effectiveness with their particular clients and communities.

Conclusion

Students cannot learn everything they need to become "super social workers" from one program—no program is perfect. Even if changes are made, gaps will still exist. At present, the authors are not convinced that social work education prepares its students for practice in the best manner possible. By extending social work graduate programs to three years of generalist studies, and by providing in-service training, seminars, and conferences for professionals, social workers can continue to be effective agents of change for the 21st century.

With present programming, social workers are not properly trained to facilitate change productively in clinical, management, and policy arenas. As a result, other professionals such as nurses, psychologists, and public health professionals might replace social workers and even make the role of the social worker obsolete. This will dramatically change how clients are served by professionals with different backgrounds and socializations. Social work students and professionals need to take a stand to promote education that will enhance their efficacy and, thus, promote the profession.

References

Bernard, D. L. (1995). *International handbook on social work education*. Westport, CT: Greenwood.

Davenport, J., & Davenport, J. (1984). Theoretical perspectives on rural/urban differences. *Human Services in the Rural Environment, 9*(1), 4-9.

Fortune, A. (1996, October). Address given at Professional Development of Helping Professions in Rural Communities, Focus Group Meeting, Albany, NY.

Hopps, J., & Collins, P. (1995). Social work profession overview. In R. L. Edwards (Ed.-in-Chief), *Encyclopedia of Social Work* (19th ed., pp. 2266-2280). Washington, DC: NASW Press.

Jones, S. J. (1996). *Working paper: Collaboration and coordination regarding rural social work and economic development*. Unpublished manuscript, State University of New York at Albany.

Orten, J., & Rich, L. (1988). A model for assessment of incestuous families. *Social Casework: The Journal of Contemporary Social Work, 69*, 611-619.

Stull, R. (1996). Finding interdisciplinary connections: A case for bringing back the generalist approach in university teaching. *National Teaching and Learning Forum, 5*(2).

Part 2

Rural Communities as a Case Study

R ural communities serve as a microcosm of the issues, concerns, and changes taking place in our society. They also provide examples of the values and strengths embedded in local communities and the types of support residents need to achieve their goals. However, the lack of a precise definition of the term *rural* and a bias toward urban policies and programs in federal and state governments leave many rural communities with problems that are inadequately addressed, such as cycles of poverty and the loss of small family farms. Helping professionals need to become advocates and use information to bring about effective change in areas of social justice, equality, and equity. As the world becomes more urbanized, many rural communities face greater economic and social hardships. This phenomenon is often found in developing countries, and rural America has been described as having 'Third World' problems (Cornelia & Christenson, 1991; Davidson, 1990).

The chapters included in this section address the significance of definitions and geography; they refer to differences within communities and how they influence federal, state, and local resources; and they introduce case studies as role models for change. In chapter 4, "Rural Health Care: A Challenge for Academic Medical Centers," Henry Pohl points out that urban and rural health care needs are similar, but their specific problems are different. Rural areas, for example, face concerns such as physician retention due to geographic isolation and diminished access to preventive services due to limited transportation. Pohl sees regional coordination as a vehicle for effective change and increased resources, and he cites Albany Medical Center as an example. The hospital is changing to a regional approach in its mission and plans for service provision and student training. The generalist practice model used by the hospital better prepares physicians to serve in nearby rural areas, and Pohl states that physicians need ongoing educational support from universities, especially in rural areas. He recommends a partnership between schools of higher education to help develop a "new reality" for urban and rural populations, discussing a proposed institute to analyze population needs, examine and promote health care planning and quality, and provide role-model education. Pohl sees telecommunications and distance learning programs as means to continuous education, training, and support for communities.

In his response to Pohl's presentation at the focus group meeting, David Smingler highlighted emerging technology and its potential benefits for rural communities. New opportunities for reaching clients with preventive and primary health care education are being developed, he reported, which offer information options that will empower clients to care for themselves and offset professional and consultant isolation. Smingler pointed out that cross-system collaboration and an interdisciplinary approach to health care may be more accepted, feasible, and more often practiced in rural than in urban areas. Partnerships between systems must occur to be able to afford services across geographic distances. Smingler also expressed concern over policies that coerce health practitioners into rural and oppressed urban areas by foregiving their loans. He also lauded policies that support aggressive dissemination of public health information into rural areas, and he discussed the costs and outcomes of preventive care, links between professionals, and a need to support successful services and programs.

Judith and Joseph Davenport concur with Pohl's concerns about the social and economic plight of rural America. In chapter 5, "Economic and Social Development and Rural Social Work as a Model of the Generalist Approach for the 21st Century," they refer to some pertinent characteristics of "rurality" and their implications for professional development. They highlight technology as a means for bringing rural social workers and their target systems into the next century. They also describe negative effects of technology, including reduction in human contact and loss of jobs due to computers and automation. The Davenports note there is no consensus definition of generalist practice, despite its historical connection to rural social work. They describe generalist practice not simply as a professional discipline, but as a way of life or means of survival. The strengths and limitations of interdisciplinary teams are also discussed in this chapter, and they cite activities at the University of Missouri–Columbia and at the Wyoming Human Services project to illustrate their conceptual material.

Anne Fortune provided a response to the Davenports' original talk at the focus group by outlining some of the problems associated with interdisciplinary endeavors. She discussed language barriers and unexamined assumptions as problems plaguing effective partnerships. A generalist model is required for rural social work, she argued, for social workers should be able to counsel families while also working with school boards and lobbying for system change. Her definition of a generalist is someone who uses an eclectic theory base rounded out with a systems model and who can intervene at every level with a planned change process.

Chapter 6, "Community-Responsive Partners for Environmental Health: Perspectives for Rural Health Professionals into the 21st Century" by Loretta Picciano, tells about new challenges in rural health due to declining incomes, decreased health benefits, and growing exposure to environmental health hazards. Picciano points out that poverty, as well as race, contributes to people's vulnerability to health risks. She states that health professionals must be prepared to identify, describe, record, treat, and prevent environmental health problems; they must also be able to address medical, political, and economic issues related to race and poverty. The author sees community collaboration with universities as a way to support communities and to prepare health and other helping professionals to meet the 21st-century challenges. She cites the work of the Rural Coalition as an example of partnerships among diverse communities that identify and address shared solutions to common problems. Environmental injustice is the current focus of the coalition, and research is one of its intervention modes for change. The author provides case studies as evidence of the scope of the problems and of how communities are working together. An interesting outcome of the projects has been the training of community researchers, she says.

Dwight Williams provides a written response to Picciano's article in the last chapter of this part. He encourages "bottom–up" participation, stating that such a strategy empowers communities, acknowledges the community's stake in the issues, and provides communities input into service definition, distribution, and access. Williams applauds the Rural Coalition model and continues a discussion of its strengths.

References

Cornelia, F., & Christenson, J. (Eds.) (1991). *Rural poliies for the 1990s* (pp. 1-7). Boulder, CO: Westview.

Davidson, O. G. (1990). *Broken heartland: The rise of America's rural ghetto* (pp. 159, 169-170). New York: Anchor.

4

Rural Health Care: A Challenge for Academic Medical Centers

Henry Pohl

> The rural health care system needs to be more coordinated. I'm an advocate of pooling resources in rural areas—avoiding unnecessary duplication. Rural hospitals need to cooperate and collaborate. (Fickenscher, 1993)

Survival, as expressed by the American Hospital Association's environmental assessment for rural hospitals in 1992 (Weisfeld, 1993):

> [To] encourage the creation of alternative delivery models for rural communities; . . . expand transportation and emergency services for isolated areas; broaden opportunities for mid-level and cross-trained practitioners; [elicit] new interest in the role of state health professional schools in encouraging rural practices; and [stimulate] the formation of telecommunication networks between small and large hospitals.

The term *rural* is usually reserved for an area that is some distance from a city. Except for this common characteristic, all rural areas are not necessarily alike. Each area has its own population base, economic foundation, and community mores. The Capital District of New York is the urban center of a 17-county area that is primarily rural and sparsely populated. The northeastern region of the state comprises about 15,380 square miles in an area over 200 miles long and 70 miles wide. The terrain in the district includes the Adirondack Mountains, the Catskill Mountains, the Hudson and Mohawk Rivers, Lake Champlain, and Lake George. Although population centers can be 5–50 miles apart, community values and peoples' individual needs are much further apart.

The health care needs of the rural population are similar to those of urban centers. Heart disease, cerebrovascular disease, cancer, and accidents are the principal causes of death. Although aging baby boomers will refocus health care needs from the young to the old, maintaining low infant mortality rates will remain a concern that necessitates comprehensive prenatal programs. The hospital-based care system of the past is quickly changing. Community physician groups are competing with hospitals as vendors of diagnostic testing, which adds to the financial instability of the rural hospital system. Solo physician practice is diminishing in the rural world as elsewhere. Insurance is moving from fee-for-service to managed care, so capitated services are no longer a future threat— they are a reality. How can a health care delivery system reorganize and stabilize with so many changing variables? How can academic medical centers act to facilitate change in this unstable environment?

Albany Medical Center is the only academic health science center in the 17-county region. The Medical Center recognized its regional role in developing its mission statement:

> Educate medical students, physicians, biomedical scientists and other health care professionals, in order to meet the future health care needs of the region and nation; foster biomedical research that leads to scientific advance and the improvement of the health of the public; and provide a broad range of patient services to the people of eastern New York and western New England, including illness-prevention programs, comprehensive care, and highly complex care associated with the academic medical centers.

The medical center has attempted to define and develop solutions to the rural health delivery dilemma. The center participated in a Robert Wood Johnson Hospital-Based Rural Hospital program with the Health Systems Agency of Northeastern New York. The center was responsible for a project aimed at retaining and recruiting health care workers using continuing education as the tool. Acknowledging the revelations of the rural health initiative, the Albany Medical College (a component of the medical center) developed a new comprehensive care four-year curriculum to encourage development of a primary or generalist care health work force.

Furthermore, the medical center's Robert Wood Johnson grant experience led to the realization that to change the face of rural health care one must alter:

• the relationship between the community and the purveyors of care

- the difficulties in recruiting and retaining health care personnel
- the role of local health care facilities
- the relationship between prevention and wellness to treating illness
- the relationship between health care professionals while they deliver care
- the integration of the continuum of care
- the role of technology in delivering and supporting care

Simply supporting the cultivation of change in rural communities is not enough. The academic medical community must help facilitate the change process and act as a stable resource to foster change. To generate sustained change, a strong partnership between government, institutions of higher learning, and the rural community is needed. Planners cannot rely on outdated history or constructs to evaluate health workforce and resource issues. Managed care and integrated health care networks have spread from urban centers to rural territories, and in doing so they have changed how providers and communities alike define problems and solutions.

The Problem

Population demographics in the United States are being altered as baby boomers move into old age. In 1987, people over the age of 64 comprised 12.2% of the population. This will rise to 13% in 2000, 21.8% in 2030, and 24.5% in 2050. More importantly, those over age 85 will grow from 9.6% of the elderly in 1987 to 15.5% in 2010. In a 1994 study that outlined the need for primary and preventive services done by the Health Systems Agency of Northeastern New York, it was reported that 17% of the population was 65 and over, whereas in New York State as a whole the number was 13% (Northeastern New York Plan, 1994). People over 65 years old use the medical system more frequently than a younger cohort. Usually older people have more chronic conditions, thereby increasing the burden on the health care system in Northeastern New York.

Poverty levels in New York's rural counties vary. Certain counties are at greater risk than others for the added problems which poverty brings to normal life (e.g., increased infant mortality, traumatic death). Local health care systems must thus work to identify and respond to their specific community needs.

Rural life in New York, like inner-city life, has been shaped by the environment and prevailing social practices. Patients in rural areas have more often opted for emergency care of severe illness than a program of ongoing preventive care. The region's geography and dramatically variable climate make access to health care over mountainous terrain difficult, as well. Although there have been great improvements in transportation over the years, coordination and availability are continual problems. Transportation issues affect patient access to preventive services, increase emergency services, and thwart some home care options.

Health care providers have generally not been enthusiastic about practicing in rural settings, because they worry about geographic isolation. Young practitioners would like to be close to the social, cultural, and professional stimulation that urban areas offer, and they want to be able to call upon a supportive network of other professionals to aid their efforts. Older physicians, too, have shunned moving to rural communities for fear of offering their children lesser educational or cultural activities. Spouses often dislike moving to a rural area due to lack of professional opportunities or social isolation.

Professional practice issues have been major deterrents to rural practice. Lack of cross-coverage and access to consultants amplify the social isolation. Practice hours become arduous. Medical education has not focused on rural practice issues either, a factor that frightened off many applicants in the past. Coordinated case-managed care is not currently the norm in American medicine. In rural locations, isolation and distance inhibit the treatment process and change the necessary dynamics.

Health Education

Many medical schools and centers are beginning to change the focus of the education they deliver, in response to reform measures endorsed by many commissions. *Physicians for the 21st Century: The Report of the Panel on the General Professional Education of the Physician and College Preparation to Medicine* (Muller, 1984) and *Healthy America: Practitioners for 2005* (Shugars, O'Neil, & Bader, 1991) are just two such influential studies. The guiding principles for medical education reform are generalizable to the needs of the whole system. Such reform should be put into the context of the health care system in general and adjusted for unique needs. Education should be measured not by program content, but by the educational outcomes or the demonstration of health care worker competencies that result from such reform.

The Pew Health Commission recommended the following competencies for practitioners by 2005 (Muller, 1984):

• *Caring for the community's health:* Practitioners should have a broad understanding of factors affecting health, such as environment, socioeconomic conditions, behavior, medical care, and genetics; they should be able to work with others in the community to generate a range of services and activities that promote, protect, and improve health.

• *Expanding access to effective care:* Practitioners should participate in efforts to improve the public's health by ensuring health care access to individuals, families, and communities.

• *Providing contemporary clinical care:* Practitioners should possess up-to-date clinical skills to meet the public's health care needs.

• *Emphasizing primary care:* Practitioners should be willing and able to function in new health care settings and interdisciplinary team arrangements designed to meet the primary health care needs of the public.

• *Participating in coordinated care:* Practitioners should be able to work effectively as team members in organized settings that emphasize high-quality, cost-effective, integrated services.

• *Ensuring cost-effective and appropriate care:* Practitioners should incorporate and balance cost and quality in the decision-making process.

• *Practicing prevention:* Practitioners should emphasize primary and secondary preventive strategies for all people.

• *Involving patients and families in the decision-making process:* Practitioners should expect patients and their families to participate actively in decisions regarding their personal health and in evaluating its quality and acceptability.

• *Promoting healthy lifestyles:* Practitioners should help individuals, families, and communities maintain and promote healthy behavior.

• *Assessing and using technology appropriately:* Practitioners should understand and apply increasingly complex and often costly technology and use it appropriately.

• *Improving the health care system:* Practitioners should understand the operations of the health care system from a broad political, economic, social, and legal perspective to continuously improve the operations and accountability of that system.

• *Managing information:* Practitioners should manage and use large volumes of scientific, technologic, and patient information.

• *Understanding the role of the physical environment:* Practitioners should be prepared to assess, prevent, and mitigate the impact of environmental hazards on the health of the population.

• *Providing counseling on ethical issues:* Practitioners should provide counseling for patients in situations where ethical issues arise and participate in discussions of ethical issues in health care as they affect communities, society, and the health profession.

• *Accommodating expanded accountability:* Practitioners should be responsive to increasing levels of public, governmental, and third-party participation in, and scrutiny of, the shape and direction of the health care system.

• *Participating in a racially diverse society:* Practitioners should appreciate the growing diversity of the population and the need to understand health status and health care through differing cultural values.

• *Continuing to learn:* Practitioners should anticipate changes in health care and respond by redefining and maintaining professional competencies through practice life.

The managed care environment requires a health care professional to acquire a more comprehensive set of competencies. This has particular relevance in rural care, especially as capitated payment becomes the norm. For example, a practitioner must understand the role of age, sex, and chronic disease on resource allocation when defining the composition of a panel of patients. The patient mix profile may bring success or failure to a practice in a sparsely populated area where flexibility is not possible. Furthermore, palliative care and end-of-life care have not been the focus of professional skill development, but in this era of managed care they take on new importance in rural areas, where alignment of teams and community resources require special attention.

Albany Medical College has begun to fulfill its responsibility to produce practitioners for 2005 prepared for a managed care framework by embracing a curriculum that encompasses all of the competencies listed above. Changing the way the traditional medical school can achieve these goals is difficult and evolutionary (rather than revolutionary). A medical school must reorganize lines of authority to restructure the educational process. At Albany, departmental responsibilities for education program components were replaced with institutional goals and programs. Programs were developed to integrate knowledge and clinical acumen. Viewing the world from a population perspective instead of from that of an individual is a new approach to health care education. To assure these goals, the medical school joined forces with a rural health care provider (Upper Hudson Primary Care Consortium in Warrensburg, NY), a health maintenance organization (Community Health Plan), and a community clinic (Whitney M. Young Jr. Health Center in Albany). Curriculum developers thought that changing the professional mindset of graduates required exposing them to as many components of the health care system as possible.

The definition of the educational campus changed to allow for the new curricular focus. The school embraced added community sites to expose students to the reality of modern medical practice. The school chose to target tertiary and critical care as components of the curriculum instead of remaining the heart of the curriculum.

These changes are occurring as the health care system evolves. Such continual flux makes changes in health care education especially difficult. The academic medical center is pitted against community hospitals and other integrated health care partners that compete for "market share." Rural areas are undergoing the same type of health system reorientation as urban areas. As practitioners in hospitals join ranks with institutions in communities large and small, where does the academic health science center sit? What should the role of the academic health science center be in this scenario? If it were to continue to champion its role as a change agent and regional resource, how could it maintain its financial base? To maintain its pivotal role in transforming the health care system, who should help secure the stability of the medical school complex? What relationship does the medical school complex have to developing integrated health care networks? In a sparsely populated area such as northeastern New York state, is the academic medical center no longer necessary to ensuring long-term and stable change?

In an invited paper in *Academic Medicine* on reform in medical education, Thomas S. Inui (1996) reiterates the importance physician competencies, but he places them in the context of an integrated care delivery system. He discusses the following practice competencies:

- information management
- care resource management
- integration of guidelines and clinical judgment
- enhanced relationships
- expanded teamwork
- management to optimal outcomes

He focuses on enhanced relationships as an overlooked competency, referencing a report that stresses the importance of good relationships between patient and provider, provider and provider, and provider and community in redefining the health care system (Tresolini & Pew–Pfizer, 1994). The relationship between the community and its health care workers has not usually been a focus of medical education, and the Pew–Pfizer Task Force outlines some of the knowledge, skills, and values that students should develop to be competent in these relationships. Rather than just create a curricular module on relationship-centered care, academic medical centers should actively pursue the necessary relationships for the community to empower individuals, families, caregivers, educators, politicians, and others to become partners in change. Here again, we run into a true dilemma: How can an academic medical center become a change agent when it must also become a market force? Who should protect the role of academic medicine as an instrument of change? Given academic medicine's past history of uncommitted social action, why should anyone champion its cause?

The Future

In the future, academic medicine must:

- define its role in the planning and development of a new health care paradigm;
- enlist the financial support of state and federal government to allow the role necessary for the stability of the health care system;
- separate itself from the market forces, while remaining part of the marketplace;
- act as a role model for all elements of the curriculum presented to students;
- fulfill institutional competencies.

Academic health science centers should not view their work in isolation. Schools of public health, social welfare, and colleges and universities might all create a blueprint of the needs of a region and work together to overcome deficits and enhance strengths. A partnership should be forged between schools of higher education to craft a new reality for both urban and rural populations. Institutes could be created to analyze population needs, focus educational programs on those needs, and develop outcome measures. The institute could become the regional arbiter for matching community needs, health care planning, and quality. Institute activities could also serve as a prototype of the team approach to problem solving—role model education at its best.

Efficient methods for delivering input and education to distant sites must be found. Albany Medical College's participation in the Robert Wood Johnson rural health grant demonstrated that health care workers can change the way they interact with one another and learn to learn. If medical schools are to promote continual learning, they must use methods of allowing experts from academic centers to interact with community physicians and other health care providers without using so much time and energy to outweigh their benefits. Consultation for clinical care problems can serve as the basis of experiential and personalized continuing education. Telecommunication and distance learning programs are ways to achieve these particular goals. Support groups of pharmacists, social workers, physical therapists, and other health care providers can meet in various sites with academic caregivers through teleconferencing technology. Curricula that help different health care workers to interact in a changing environment can be enhanced through controlled distance learning programs. Databases and educational programs can be made available to the general public through independent learning centers or virtual libraries housed in academic centers. Patients in communities, then, can be considered students of the academic health science centers, empowering them to begin to understand health, illness prevention, and interaction with health care providers. The community and the health care system must determine outcome measures that will be used to maintain a quality patient-centered rural care system. An active program of interprofessional communication can also be enhanced by maintaining relationships over long distances. This will help local relationships build into regional relationships, which build into statewide relationships—the development of a true system.

References

Inui, T. S. (1996). Reform in medical education: A health of the public perspective. *Academic Medicine, 71*(Suppl. 1), 119-121.

Muller, S. (1984). *Physicians for the 21st century: The report of the Panel on the General Professional Education of the Physician and College Preparation to Medicine.* Washington, DC: Association of American Medical Colleges.

Northeastern New York Plan for Primary and Preventive Health Care. (1994, January). Health Systems Agency of Northeastern New York.

Shugars, D. A., O'Neil, E. H., & Bader, J. D. (1991). Healthy America: Practitioners for 2005, An agenda for action for U.S. health professional schools. Durham, NC: Pew Health Professions Commission.

Tresolini, C. P., & Pew–Pfizer Task Force on Relationship-Centered Care. (1994). *Health professions education and relationship-centered care.* San Francisco: Pew Health Professions Commission.

Weisfeld, J. D. (1993). *Rural health challenges in the 1990s—Strategies from the hospital-based rural health care program.* Princeton, NJ: Robert Wood Johnson Foundation.

5

Economic and Social Development and Rural Social Work as a Model of the Generalist Approach for the 21st Century

Judith A. Davenport and Joseph Davenport III

Addressing the focus group topic "Professional Development of Helping Professions in Rural Communities" is a challenging and interesting proposition, especially when a major objective is to integrate economic and social development and technology into the equation. Describing professional practice in rural areas is neither an easy nor precise task. From a romantic perspective, "rural" may connote an idyllic Eden populated by bucolic farm families with close family and community ties and living in harmony with the land. Such a perspective, often commercialized, can be found on television (e.g., "Mayberry RFD," "The Waltons") and in numerous country music songs lamenting the loss of a simpler life. Another portrait, however paradoxical, shows rural communities as foreboding, sinister places filled with degenerates and hiding deep and terrible secrets. Characters from William Faulkner's novels, James Dickey's *Deliverance*, and movies such as *Mississippi Burning* are just a few examples. The truth, as in most cases, includes both extremes and considerably more in between (Davenport & Davenport, 1995).

Social scientists have developed various definitions of "rural" and various theories to explain rural–urban differences. Because of this variety, social workers and others might define and approach strengths and problems differently. Several generally accepted aspects of rurality are important to mention, however, in any discussion of rural economic and social development and of human services training and practice. Some pertinent *economic* characteristics distilled from several authors (Davenport & Davenport, 1995; Deavers, 1992; Hassinger & Hobbs, 1992) include:

- More rural communities are farming-dependent than manufacturing-dependent, although manufacturing constitutes the primary source of export earnings.
- Rural communities tend to have specialized economies, often relying on one economic base related to natural resources (e.g., agriculture, mining, forestry).
- The service economy is growing faster than any other segment.
- Geographic location creates social and economic problems due to physical remoteness and social and cultural isolation.
- Rural areas do not tend to be integrated into centers of information, innovation, technology, and finance.
- Rural residents tend to be poorer and less educated, perform jobs that are hazardous, and have fewer resources such as health insurance than their urban counterparts.
- The nature of 'doing business' is less formalized, more personal, and tends to have more of a social component than business transactions conducted in urban areas.

Some salient *social* characteristics, both positive and negative, that need to be considered for human services practice (Davenport & Davenport, 1982; Ginsberg, 1993; Jones, 1993; Martinez-Brawley, 1990) include:

- Most social work and human services activities are handled in small agencies in the public sector. Workers are relatively isolated, confront a multitude of complex problems, and frequently lack access to specialized services. The "devolution revolution" may change this as private companies move into the managed care and welfare arenas. Also, time limits on public assistance will add extra responsibilities on workers who must find and develop employment opportunities.
- Rural areas face a shortage of other human service professionals; those that do exist are often overburdened and possess limited resources.
- Rural residents usually evaluate human service professionals by the help they deliver or problems they solve, rather than by their educational level, professional orientation, credentials, or diplomas from prestigious universities.

- Informal relationships are powerful, can be extremely beneficial, and must be understood and used appropriately.
- Clients and workers experience lack of anonymity, or "life in a goldfish bowl."
- Professionals, especially those who come from urban areas, may encounter value conflicts with people who are more conservative and traditional. Dual relationships between workers and clients may be almost unavoidable, and these can create ethical dilemmas.
- Confidentiality issues are different in small towns, where personal contacts are frequent in everyday pursuits and clients are identified if they park by the agency or if the worker visits their home.
- Many rural communities have a more diverse population than might be expected. Professionals expecting a homogeneous population are often surprised by this, but Josephine Brown (1933) pointed out over 60 years ago that rural people and communities vary greatly. For example, consider the different ethnic, cultural, religious, social, gender, class, age, and socioeconomic variables in the following groups: Missouri Amish, Louisiana Cajun, Wyoming Basque, New Mexico Pueblo, Alaska Aleut, North Carolina Hmong, Utah Mormon, Atlantic Coast Gullah, Mississippi Delta African American, Southwestern TexMex, Tennessee auto worker, Georgia poultry factory worker, California counterculture member, and New York migrant worker. The list could go indefinitely; hence, the professional should be prepared to encounter and work with clients from diverse backgrounds.
- Many rural communities have a high percentage of dependent populations, both young and old. It is not uncommon for areas to have an elderly population exceeding 20% as younger people move for employment opportunities. Also, some rural areas have become retirement meccas, such as the North Georgia mountains.

Technology and Rural Areas

Although rural areas have lagged behind their urban counterparts in plugging into the emerging information age, an increasing number are realizing that technology will be an important part of their economic future. According to Macarov (1991) in *Certain Change: Social Work Practice in the Future*, both the opportunities for economic and social development and advances in technology are astonishing. The issue of locality might have less relevance in an age of information and worldwide marketing. With the proper equipment, the information age can be accessed by anyone, anywhere. Technology will also accentuate and accelerate the already important service industry in rural locales.

Marginal groups, which are prevalent in many rural environments, will have more opportunities to take advantage of these technological breakthroughs. Social workers and others must diligently ensure that all groups are included in planning for, preparing for, and taking advantage of the new opportunities. More elderly and disabled residents can live more independently with motorized wheelchairs, pagers, cell phones, alarm systems, voice-activated household appliances, and the internet. These resources will become easier to use, more efficient, and more beneficial, and they need to be made available.

Despite the expansion of technological remedies, there will still be a need for direct contact with people, especially those who are housebound. Many problems that come to the attention of human service personnel are related to feelings of isolation and lack of human contact. The elderly and infirm still need visitation. Technology is a supplement to human beings, not a substitute. Additionally, cases of abuse and neglect require on-the-scene observation, which cannot be replicated with present technology.

Macarov (1991) lists six ways that technology can help social workers in practice:

- agency management—record keeping, filing, etc.
- case management—tracking client demographics and clinical data
- policy and planning—following statistics and trends
- research goals
- direct service to clients—using diagnostic instruments, intake assessments, etc.
- interactive therapeutic programs

Additional benefits include the use of telecommunications (e.g., satellites, fiber optics) for direct work with clients and for consultation on difficult cases from a specialist or supervisor at a regional location. (Telemedicine has been a good model for such programs; see Alonzi, 1996.) Telecommunications is also useful for interdisciplinary and interagency collaborations and as a means of delivering degree programs, continuing education, and additional credentialing requirements. Again, technology will be a supplement to such enterprises, not a substitute. Rural workers will still want to attend actual conferences, and adult educators know the value of a controlled environment free of interruptions or distractions which too much technology can bring.

Disadvantages to the increased use of technology include replacing people with equipment in locations where employment is limited, and problems with financing and updating computer businesses, securing adequate computer repair services in a sparsely populated and isolated locale, and paying for toll costs to "help lines." The electronic world can also be dehumanizing. Some professionals who spend endless hours on computers lose direct contact with people. And when a social worker's communication skills become stilted, follow-up questions might not always be asked and nonverbal signals can be missed. Additionally, rural residents who did not grow up with advanced technology might feel uncomfortable and resistant to it.

Generalist Practice

The task of utilizing technology to its fullest in practice while also addressing community problems requires an examination of the roles of the rural social worker and human service worker. Historical and current professional literature support the practice wisdom that the nature and context of rural practice requires the generalist model for most settings. In fact, the benefits of being a generalist jack-of-all-trades is not confined to professional disciplines. Instead, it is recognized as a way of life or a means of survival—a farmer might have to be an electrician, plumber, money manager, or whatever is needed to maintain the farm.

Although there is no single agreed-upon definition of generalist practice, Schatz, Jenkins, and Sheafor (1990, p. 223) state that:

> Generalist social work is one way of viewing practice, that is, a perspective focusing on the interface between systems with equal emphasis on the goals of social justice, humanizing systems, and improving the well-being of people .... The initial level of generalist practice consists of five elements: . . . the Generic foundation . . . a multilevel problem-solving methodology . . . a multiple, theoretical orientation . . . a knowledge, value, and skill base that is transferable between and among diverse contexts and locations . . . an open assessment unconstricted by any particular theoretical approach.

Landon (1995, p. 1103) notes that:

> There appears to be definitional agreement on the centrality of the multimethod and multilevel approaches, based on an eclectic choice of theory base and the necessity for incorporating the dual vision of the profession or private issues and social justice concerns.

Utilizing a generalist approach to rural practice certainly has an honored heritage. Davenport and Davenport (1984, 1996) have found that social work pioneers such as Josephine Brown and Eduard Lindeman were describing generalist practice shortly after the turn of the century. Brown's classic *The Rural Community and Social Casework* (1933) might sound like a single-method approach, but she described the social caseworker as one who must use group and community interventions when needed. Lindeman's work might commonly be associated with urban New York, but he first practiced in rural Michigan. His seminal work, *The Community: An Introduction to the Study of Leadership and Organization* (1921), describes a rural social worker who applies different strategies to a variety of client systems. Eschewing a narrow technical definition of practice, these early rural social workers sought both individual and social change within the context of social justice. Ecological and systems terms may not have been used, but their concepts were evident.

By definition, the generalist can serve many roles requisite for rural practice, including those of therapist, planner, administrator, consultant, and community organizer and developer (McMahon, 1990). While this model has been of historical importance for rural practice, it has become increasingly important for urban and inner-city practice, where the health care industry, in particular, is rapidly embracing it. One caveat is that utilizing the generalist model as the backbone of the service delivery system does not eliminate the need for specialists. Rural mental health workers might be generalists, but specialists should be available, when needed, through such mechanisms as circuit riders, mobile clinics, and telecommunications networks. The generalist's extensive knowledge of group and organizational behavior, group work (especially task groups), conflict resolution and mediation skills, community resources, and policy formulation and change makes social work an ideal profession for interdisciplinary leadership in these areas.

Interdisciplinary Collaboration

A scarcity of helping professionals, combined with a high volume of work and lack of resources, strongly support the belief that interdisciplinary collaboration is not only desired but necessary in rural America as we approach the 21st century. As stated in *Social Work: An Empowering Profession* (Dubois & Miley, 1992, p. 222), the communication, collaboration, and consolidation of knowledge involved in interdisciplinary teamwork "is a transactional process, out of which evolves a totality that is greater than that which can be achieved by any of the individuals working along or alone in summation."

Such collaboration is not new to social work. Social workers in the Charity Organization Societies invented the case conference in the 1880s as a means of bringing together different workers to share information and jointly plan for clients. The profession has had its own agencies staffed primarily by social workers, but it has also been a secondary discipline in hospitals, prisons, and other institutions. Social work's emphasis on the total person-in-environment made it an ideal discipline for bringing people together to share information, brainstorm, and develop intervention strategies.

Interdisciplinary teamwork offers many positive outcomes, but there can be drawbacks. Inequality of team members is sometimes discussed in the literature. Sheafor, Horejsi, and Horejsi (1988) argue, however, that professional inequality can occur when one profession is able to devote more time than others to collaborative initiatives. Collaboration might save resources, but each discipline must begin with an adequate resource base. Social work sometimes suffers because it does not generally enjoy a large resource base, even though its range of activities is broad. For example, social work is considered a core discipline in health, mental health, schools, corrections, substance abuse, and family service areas. The senior author of this chapter represents her school of social work on many interdisciplinary faculty teams. If the school does not send a representative, it will be left "out of the loop" by default. Its unique expertise could be lost while other professions, for which there is less demand, may seize an opportunity to expand their turf simply because they possess the time and resources to retool and redefine their disciplines for roles and tasks historically occupied by social work. This does not mean, however, that they perform the job as well.

Professions such as social work and nursing which struggle for autonomy are most likely to come into conflict with others. In addition, similarities to other disciplines' identities and roles tend to generate more conflict. It is easier for social workers to define roles with physical therapists than with psychologists or even nurses.

Collaboration can sometimes result in strain if a task is technical and highly specialized. Generalized task work might be best suited for such activities since the specialized task can be better dealt with alone (Compton & Galaway, 1989). Collaborative efforts can also be meccas for obstructionists who can use their knowledge to delay and even deny group processes, especially if they are knowledgeable about human behavior in general and group behavior when meeting in teams.

Nontenured faculty may have problems securing tenure by being involved in interdisciplinary education. Our experience at several universities has taught us that universities frequently do not reward, and indeed penalize, interdisciplinary work. Rewards are greater for grants brought into the school than for involvement in someone else's grant, which pits disciplines against each other and hinders collaboration. Greater efforts must be made to change this system, especially at Research I universities.

The "devolution revolution" is another powerful force contributing to an increase in interdisciplinary work (Abramson & Rosenthal, 1995). Republican congressional victories in the 1994 and 1996 elections, along with more centrist policies from President Clinton, have pushed policy and programs toward state and local levels of government, where scarce resources demand teamwork without costly duplication. Service consumers are also increasingly demanding a role and function in the team process.

Interdisciplinary teams capture much of the professional attention in interdisciplinary collaboration, but they are not the only mechanisms. Interdisciplinary training is another important area (Casto & Julia, 1994). Teaching and modeling this behavior in higher education is imperative if graduates are expected to practice it. Professional lip service without action will not suffice.

The School of Social Work at the University of Missouri–Columbia faces not just opportunities but expectations for interdisciplinary involvement. It is a means of survival in higher education today and will be more so tomorrow. Many grants now require interdisciplinary efforts. Examples of current endeavors include three behavioral health groups, two physical health groups, a geriatric group, and a caring communities/schools project.

Involvement with these diverse groups is both rewarding and irritating. Benefits are often extolled while drawbacks are ignored or minimized. However, chances for successful training can be improved if attention is paid to potential negatives.

The University of Missouri–Columbia's school of social work has prided itself, and been lauded by administrative and community sectors, for its land-grant successes in meeting the needs of students from across the state. Its curriculum is "commuter-friendly," featuring evening and weekend classes, but none on Fridays. Each of the school's training partners wants this schedule changed to match theirs. Hence, social work faculty and students are the only disciplinary participants who must participate in this course during the time they have scheduled for research and other scholarly activities. Moreover, the faculty member assigned to the grant is a nontenured instructor who must give up her research day to be part of this project. On the other hand, the block placement in the second year meets social work needs, but not those of other disciplines.

Another difficulty arises for the school when other disciplines want MSW students for interdisciplinary training with their bachelor-level counterparts (e.g., in education, nursing, health-related professions). Cross-listing courses that span different levels of education can be a problem in academic settings; accreditation standards also limit the types of courses other disciplines can take.

Other problems stem from different disciplinary foci, cultures, terminologies, values, modus operandi, and long-term animosities. Some health care professionals have operated in a medical model and are used to issuing orders, resulting in medical and nursing students being assigned to placements against their wishes. Schools of social work do not operate like this. Hidden agendas in interdisciplinary interactions must be recognized and dealt with, for much time can be lost while people jockey for position and resources within the collaborative structure.

As mentioned earlier, modeling interdisciplinary behavior in higher education and in the workplace is a necessity. It is appalling that some students can graduate in a helping discipline without knowing that social workers are the primary providers of mental and behavioral health services. Some do not even realize that social workers provide mental and behavioral health services at all. To be charitable, some disciplines (e.g., psychology) offer internships in clinics operated and staffed primarily by members of that discipline. Their students may receive a more limited perspective on behavioral health practice than do other perspectives, such as social work and nursing, whose students are placed in the "real world" where interdisciplinary practice is a routine occurrence. Still, one must question a discipline's commitment to interdisciplinary practice if it fails to teach students the roles and functions of the core mental health professions.

Acknowledging the proper roles and functions of other disciplines is not only ethically appropriate, but highly desirable for developing trust. Team members must take risks when exposing themselves, and this is more easily accomplished in an atmosphere of trust. Trust is extremely helpful when dealing with delicate areas of role blurring. In fact, trust may allow an admission that a particular person or profession is not the most suitable for a task or function. Lack of trust can impede or even torpedo interdisciplinary efforts. This is especially true in rural communities, where helping personnel tend to remain in positions a long time and the collective memory is strong. An untrustworthy person may "poison the well" for years for a particular agency or discipline, sometimes leaving a newcomer with no choice but to labor mightily to overcome a predecessor.

When all is said and done, we have to remember that interdisciplinary teams are still comprised of individual personalities. The individual, not the agency or profession, makes the greatest difference in rural locales. And when clients and communities need help, they do not necessarily care about specific degrees, levels of degrees, or where they were acquired; respect is accorded those who establish the program, provide the service, and simply get the job done.

The Wyoming Human Services Project

Case examples are often a valuable means of illustrating conceptual and theoretical material. This chapter concludes with such an example from an NIMH-funded project that became a model for rural communities in the U.S. and numerous other countries. It is an example of rural generalist practice addressing economic and social development from an interdisciplinary perspective (Davenport & Davenport, 1979, 1980).

During the international energy crisis of the 1970s, oil shortages and spiraling energy prices created massive economic dislocations in Western countries heavily dependent on imported oil. Locating, developing, and transporting domestic energy supplies became a national priority. Rural America, particularly the Rocky Mountain West, faced massive changes from energy projects developing oil, gas, uranium, hydroelectric, thermal, coal, coal gasification, and solar projects. Hundreds, possibly thousands, of small towns went from quiet rural cultures to bustling boom towns.

The nation appreciated the energy supplies, state governments welcomed the tax revenues, and development-minded chamber of commerce–types prepared for "heaven on earth." But a funny thing happened on the path to economic nirvana. The social consequences of rapid development had not been adequately anticipated, considered, or planned for. Communities turned upside down in the vortex of change and the quality of life wilted. Social indices went through the roof with startling increases in alcohol problems, child abuse and domestic violence, and criminal activities. Human reactions to the overwhelming rate of change and economic development became predictable enough to coin a new malady: the Gillette Syndrome, named for the infamous Wyoming boom town.

The uneven balance between economic and social development had dramatic effects in Rock Springs, Wyoming. Energy companies saw initial profits dwindle as personnel turnover passed 100% annually; new workers were constantly being recruited and trained at great expense, and current workers were inefficient due to personal and family problems. People said that the two prettiest sights in Wyoming were the Grand Tetons in the front car window and Rock Springs in the rear window!

Energy companies, not usually known for their altruism, began hiring social workers, health personnel, recreation specialists, and others to mitigate the problems. Other state governments began devoting resources, too. At the University of Wyoming, professors from social work, psychology, communications, anthropology, sociology, geography, nursing, and medicine began an informal series of meetings to share their perspectives on dealing with the crisis. These efforts led to a more formal approach toward interdisciplinary cooperation and planning. A grant application resulted in the NIMH-funded Wyoming Human Services Project (WHSP) for training, applied research, and consultation. The WHSP, initially located in the College of Human Medicine, employed a full-time director (the senior author of this chapter), field director, research associate, and secretary, and engaged numerous professors on a part-time basis. Students from 29 majors took two newly created classes on impact mitigation and competed to be members of interdisciplinary teams in boom towns following graduation. The classes, special seminars, field trips, and retreats included content on the nature of energy development, community and social development, problem-solving skill development, team building and group work, and grantsmanship.

Communities interested in teams had to secure funding (e.g., from energy companies or local governments) and provide sites. The teams had a time limit for their projects—a key selling point in conservative, anti-bureaucratic, anti-government, rural locales. Interestingly enough, most team members were hired in the communities after the project ended, a significant and unintended outcome. Moreover, community willingness to fund the program teams is an example of how professional development may be funded at a time of federal retrenchment.

Team members spent half of their time relieving overburdened agency personnel, such as social workers in mental health centers, nurses in public health offices, and attorneys in prosecutor's offices. The other half was spent in community development efforts, such as school programs to prevent boom town bifurcation, employment strategies to include women and minorities in economic development, and religious efforts aimed at outreach and inclusion of newcomers. In social work projects, team members had agency supervision, advisory board input, and consultation and supervision from the university-based field director.

Interdisciplinary activities, though relatively common today, were not nearly as ubiquitous 20 years ago. Disciplines like social work, psychology, and nursing had considerable experience in collaboration, but other disciplines were worlds apart. Formal and informal planning emphasized not only goals, but member contributions and their ability to work together. Myths and stereotypes had to be identified, confronted, and dispelled. Social work was more than "welfare work," sociologists weren't just "ivory tower" intellectuals, nurses weren't just "handmaidens" to physicians, and business majors weren't just "greedy capitalists" consumed by the bottom line. Some of the more effective informal mechanisms included sharing coffee at the student union, beers at the Cowboy Bar, and exercising together.

As might be expected, developing and teaching students from 29 majors was no easy task. Initial activities included students sharing information about themselves, their disciplines, and what they hoped to achieve. Knowledge and appreciation of each other's disciplines emerged. Instructors contributed to this process by further explaining their disciplines and role-modeling interdisciplinary actions. Differences were acknowledged, while a focus on participants' shared goals provided a unifying force. Of particular importance was the strong belief in promoting positive development in Wyoming communities. Students were primarily from Wyoming and did not want their hometowns to become another Gillette or Rock Springs. Even conservative groups across the state acknowledged the need for more than just all-out economic development. The fact that team members were from Wyoming also aided their acceptance by small towns often suspicious of "outside experts," especially those from the federal government and universities.

Students received considerable exposure to troubled communities and interpersonal relationship skills. General group concepts, techniques, and exercises were used to prepare people for a variety of planning and support groups. Team building and conflict resolution were of major importance. Another area of value included community planning, development, and organization. Locating formal and informal resources, including natural helping systems, was emphasized, as was developing new resources when necessary.

References

Abramson, J. S., & Rosenthal, B. B. (1995). Interdisciplinary and interorganizational collaboration. In R. L. Edwards (Ed.-in-Chief), *Encyclopedia of social work* (19th ed., pp. 1479-1469). Washington, DC: NASW Press.

Alonzi, D. (1996). *Technology in the human services.* Paper presented at the 21st National Institute on Social Work and Human Services in Rural Areas, Kalamazoo, MI.

Brown, J. C. (1933). *The rural community and social casework.* New York: Family Welfare Association of America.

Casto, R. M., & Julia, M. C. (1994). *Interprofessional care and collaborative practice.* Pacific Grove, CA: Brooks/Cole.

Compton, B., & Galaway, B. (1989). *Social work process.* Belmont, CA: Wadsworth.

Davenport, J., & Davenport, J. A. (Eds.). (1980). *The boom town: Problems and promises in the energy vortex.* Laramie, WY: University of Wyoming Press.

Davenport, J., & Davenport, J. A. (1984). Josephine Brown's classic book still guides rural social work. *Social Casework, 65*(7), 413-419.

Davenport, J., & Davenport, J. A. (1996). *Eduard C. Lindeman's "The Community": A diamond anniversary retrospective on its contributions to rural social work.* Paper presented at the 21st National Institute on Social Work and the Human Services in Rural Areas, Kalamazoo, MI.

Davenport, J. A., & Davenport, J. (Eds.). (1979). *Boom towns and human services.* Laramie, WY: University of Wyoming Press.

Davenport, J. A., & Davenport, J. (1982). Utilizing the social network in rural communities. *Social Casework, 63*(2), 106-113.

Davenport, J. A., & Davenport, J. (1995). Rural social work overview. In R. L. Edwards (Ed.-in-Chief), *Encyclopedia of social work* (19th ed., pp. 2076-2085). Washington, DC: NASW Press.

Deavers, K. (1992). What is rural? *Policy Studies Journal, 20*(2), 183-189.

Dubois, B., & Miley, K. K. (1992). *Social work: An empowering profession.* Boston: Allyn and Bacon.

Ginsberg, L. H. (1993). *Social work in rural communities* (2nd ed.). Alexandria, VA: Council on Social Work Education.

Hassinger, E. W., & Hobbs, D. J. (1992). Rural society: The environment of rural health care. In L. A. Straub & N. Walzer (Eds.), *Rural health care: Innovation in a changing environment* (pp. 178-190). Westport, CT: Praeger.

Jones, S. (1993). *Sociocultural and services issues in working with rural clients.* Albany, NY: Nelson A. Rockefeller College of Public Affairs and Policy.

Landon, P. S. (1995). Generalist and advanced generalist practice. In R. L. Edwards (Ed.-in-Chief), *Encyclopedia of social work* (19th ed., pp. 1101-1108). Washington, DC: NASW Press.

Lindeman, E. C. (1921). *The community: An introduction to the study of community leadership and organization.* New York: Association Press.

Macarov, D. (1991). *Certain change: Social work practice in the future.* Silver Spring, MD: NASW Press.

Martinez-Brawley, E. E. (1990). *Perspectives on the small community: Humanistic views for practitioners.* Silver Spring, MD: NASW Press.

McMahon, M. D. (1990). *The general method of social work practice: A problem solving approach.* Englewood Cliffs, NJ: Prentice Hall.

Schatz, M., Jenkins, L., & Sheafor, B. (1990). Milford redefined: A model of initial and advanced generalist social work. *Journal of Education for Social Work, 26*(3), 217-231.

Sheafor, B. W., Horejsi, C. R., & Horejsi, G. A. (1991). *Techniques and guidelines for social work practice* (2nd ed.). Boston: Allyn and Bacon.

6

Community-Responsive Partners for Environmental Health: Perspectives for Rural Health Professionals into the 21st Century

Lorette Picciano

The Rural Coalition/Coalición Rural is a culturally diverse alliance of nearly 100 community-based member groups promoting just and sustainable development in the rural United States and Mexico.[1] Since 1978 the Coalition has worked with groups representing the poor and people of color—including farmworkers groups, indigenous communities, and African-American and other minority farmers—to share strategies and support one another in promoting sustainable rural development. By the late 1980s, these groups identified the health status of their constituent communities as a major issue as well as the need for better information on the impact of exposure to local environmental hazards and the impact of rural development alternatives proposed in their communities.

Scientists and health professionals had long been viewed as opposing such efforts, and Rural Coalition (RC) members worked for years to develop partnerships with scientists and health providers willing to look at issues from the perspective of, and in partnership with, community-based organizations. The "Community-Responsive Partners for Environmental Health Project of the Rural

---

[1] The Rural Coalition and its 90 culturally and regionally diverse grassroots members are committed to grassroots-directed, practical solutions to benefit members and promote long-term shared pursuit of equity and collaboration. The RC Board is elected by its membership and reflects it diversity. It meets biannually and is accountable to the membership. An annual assembly brings together over 200 participants. As a nongovernmental organization, the coalition is governed on shared principles of participatory democracy, transparency, and accountability, which it seeks to see mirrored in the institutions that govern our lives.

Coalition," funded by the National Institute of Environmental Health Sciences (NIEHS), networks rural communities, environmental health research scientists and institutions, and local health providers in a collaborative effort to address environmental health issues among populations facing disproportionate hazards. This program has built collaborative efforts that prepare all participants for the health challenges ahead. Year One outcomes provide a unique perspective on both needs and strategies to be addressed by helping professions in rural areas as they prepare to work with communities in the next century (see Marentes et al., 1996).

New Challenges in Rural Health

Rural communities face declining incomes, decreased health benefits, reduced access to services, growing exposure to environmental health hazards, and increasing rates of environmental illness. Economic conditions spark reductions in health services and health status, increased pressure to accept new environmentally hazardous industries, declining infrastructure and cleanup of existing hazards, lack of environmental health training among health professionals, and other conditions that make health delivery and promotion ever more important.

Rural health professionals must thus be equipped to identify, describe, record, treat, and prevent environmental health problems; they must be able to address the medical, political, and economic issues inherent to these conditions; and they must develop community-wide approaches to serve at-risk and vulnerable rural populations. The prevalence of environmental hazards in rural communities requires a considerable enhancement of skills and access to information. Environmental health training should be a basic component for rural health professionals in the coming century.

A multidisciplinary approach to defining the health status of the community and its vulnerable populations, and an assessment of community industries and hazards likely to affect health, will prepare professionals to identify and better respond to potential disease patterns. Collaboration among health professionals and researchers is particularly important in certain emerging areas of research. Researchers are only beginning to grapple with devising research methods to study the impact of exposures to high levels of toxic mixtures, which, when combined, might have far greater impact on people's health than single exposures. Because exposure patterns include a growth of such mixtures in rural areas, health professionals can play a vital role in learning how such exposures can lead to disease patterns.

Frequently, vulnerable health status and high exposures are features of the poorest and most uninsured populations, including farmworkers and poor and minority communities with environmentally hazardous industries. Health care training alone, however, cannot address every aspect of protecting public health. Collaboration with community groups is also essential for gaining access to populations and tackling issues that are played out in the political and economic arena. Thus, the formation of teams of researchers, health professionals, and community groups provides a basic level of essential skills needed to improve health in rural areas.

The Rural Coalition project focuses on communities where the multidisciplinary approach is essential. In Columbia, Mississippi, for example, environmental illnesses contracted by elderly residents of a public housing project built at the site of a chemical plant explosion cannot be alleviated by medical care alone. Their symptoms are unlikely to be addressed through cleanup efforts, and economic and political intervention must be used if a more healthy environment is to be provided.

Partnerships and Potential

Partnerships among diverse communities built upon shared understandings and goals have been a hallmark of the Rural Coalition since its inception. The goal of shared work has helped communities to identify and prioritize potential allies and to assess their willingness to work on an equal basis with low-income groups in the Rural Coalition. The need for research and analysis on environmental health hazards motivated the RC to seek new allies in the health and research communities. Current work indicates that community collaboration with universities, health providers, and the public sector has great potential for generating effective methods to identify and address the significant problems faced by rural at-risk populations.

Groups join the RC to find shared understanding and experience with others facing not only severe economic and environmental problems, but also racism, hostility, and neglect from the larger society. These linkages outside the community are vital in building groups' confidence and connections.

Current Work on Environmental Injustice

We are writing to you to ask for your help. We were working in the fields. As usual, the owner did not have the bottled water for us that is part of the law. So we had to drink from the ditch. We know this water has many pesticides. But there was nothing else. We drank it. The next day we were sick. Because we missed a day of work, we were fired.

Letter from farmworker to June 1996 Binational Pesticides Workshop[2]

Since the 1980s, Rural Coalition members have confronted situations of environmental injustice. Late in the decade, the RC Native 'American Task Force helped indigenous communities design and conduct a study of contaminated groundwater. Their findings compared similar communities of relatives with and without primary pollution sources, and the results led to negotiations that forced the federal government to truck in bottled water at no cost to the community. Young women who learned to collect water samples entered health professions (one became a doctor), and this methodology was shared with over a dozen similar communities in other nations.

Currently, the RC environmental justice project seeks to articulate the health needs not only of individuals, but of the community. Other strategies used might include methods to map the community for hazards, disease patterns, and locations of temporary and special needs groups. Developing the project took several years, as relationships were nurtured among diverse populations. The initial interactions between community activists and scientists were tentative and the lack of trust and confidence evident. But impetus from government agencies advocating community outreach opened new avenues for cooperation, as did the formation of networks among scientists and community members who shared a belief that environmental hazards posed real and significant health dangers.

The RC project emerged after a meeting between Health and Environment Committee chairperson Patricia Bellanger and Dr. Eula Bingham, former administrator of the Occupational Health and Safety Institute. Each woman called upon networks of relationships with key colleagues. A fall 1994 meeting convened RC mem-

---

[2] Presented to "Collaborative Partnerships with Farmworkers and Families: Pesticides, Agriculture and Environmental Justice on the U.S.–Mexico Border," Rural Coalition–sponsored conference, June 14–16, 1996, at Centro de Trabajadores Agricolas Fronterizos, El Paso, TX.

bers from poor communities and research scientists from several NIEHS–funded environmental health centers. Participants designed a joint research project that won a four-year grant from NIEHS for the Rural Coalition and its affiliates to create more partnerships among members.

Participating scientists report that their research has been informed and enhanced by collaborating with the communities which invite their expertise, and they find personal reward in knowing their skills make a real difference to the communities. Health providers are also a key to strengthening relationships among communities and scientists, and those who participated say their clinical skills and confidence in diagnosing environmentally related illnesses have been enhanced through collaboration with the scientists. When three different networks of partners with little collaborative experience come together, their work requires careful attention, but the respect and benefits that emerge seem well worth the effort in this four-year endeavor.

Community-Responsive Partners Project Structure

The project structure has two basic elements: (a) a National Advisory Board, which convenes representatives of researchers, health professionals, and communities, and (b) local projects, which model the kind of collaboration proposed. The board monitors emerging projects and the quality of the relationships among participants; addresses accountability issues; develops new strategic collaborations and funding avenues to match the interests of scientists and communities; participates in evaluation and outreach efforts to review progress and achievements; and communicates results in a strategic manner.

The following two model projects illustrate where scientists and communities have rolled up their sleeves and begun work. Each has formed a local advisory board to enhance collaboration among all partners in the ongoing work.

The Sumter County Project

The Atlanta-based Federation of Southern Cooperatives (FSC) has worked for over 25 years to meet the needs of African-American farmers through credit unions and cooperative marketing. FSC's training center in Epes, Alabama, is less than 25 miles from the largest toxic dump in the United States, owned and operated by

Chemical Waste Corporation. Sumter and Greene counties share the dump site, have a predominately African-American population, and rank among the poorest counties in the nation. Racial tensions remain high; four local African-American churches were burned in late 1995 and early 1996.

Nearby residents have long sought to ascertain if this toxic dump has had an impact on the health of the community. A veil of silence has met almost every attempt to learn more about the impact of environmental hazards associated with the dump, where up to 100 tractor-trailer loads of waste are deposited daily. A wide variety of toxic materials are allowed, including waste removed from Superfund sites around the nation. Workers in the facility are required to use the company doctor, and medical reports have not been independently examined. Cancer rates in the counties are among the highest in the state. Many long-term health hazards are also difficult to track, because they might not exhibit themselves until after workers hired from outside the community return to other locales, such as rural Mississippi. The FSC recruited a local physician, who directs local health service programs, and a toxicologist and other environmental health researchers from New Jersey–based Environmental and Occupational Health and Safety Institute (EOHSI) to seek answers to the community's questions concerning the dump. Although geographic proximity would logically dictate scientific partners from Alabama be used, the community felt that Chemical Waste Corporation might have "bought" the scientific expertise at local universities through large donations. In this case, geographic distance was an asset, and participating scientists committed themselves to scientific integrity and full disclosure to the community.

In July and August 1996, the project physician received clinical training in environmental and occupational medicine supported by EOHSI. She worked closely with scientists and the community as proposals for a research agenda were developed. The team has developed a much keener awareness of the political nature of the work and the myriad concerns that communities must balance. Initial reports indicate enthusiasm from all partners, with one scientist noting, "This is the best thing we've done." Although it is certainly a research challenge to isolate hazards among the many chemicals dumped in Sumter County, the team is also focusing on how the compromised health status of a low-income African-American community increases vulnerability to exposures from environmental contamination with potential for adverse health outcomes.

The team in Alabama has already conducted several training sessions for community members in scientific methods. New methods of reporting health problems are being reviewed, as are medical statistics for the county before and after the dump was built two decades ago. The community members will be trained to collect samples for analysis, with a larger research grant now being sought.

The Binational Pesticides Project

The Rural Coalition's second model project serves migrant farmworkers on the U.S.–Mexico border. The farmworker organization collaborated with the city of El Paso, Texas, after a long struggle to build a center for the workers, who previously slept on streets, awaiting labor contractors. Now they have cots, lockers, showers, health services, a cafeteria, alcohol and drug abuse counseling, and training on issues of concern. Scientists are designing assessments of pesticide exposure of the workers on both sides of the border. The Farmworker Health and Safety Institute, based in Glassboro, New Jersey, and run by several area farmworker groups, conducts seminars that certify workers as trainers in EPA worker protection standards. The training and the emerging research focuses on pesticides, their health impact, and what can farmworkers do to recognize and prevent illness.

Preliminary Findings

Because the diverse participants were involved as partners in the initial design, early reservations and suspicions continue to be overcome, and differences in value systems are being viewed as strengths and opportunities for learning. The need for networking, training, and routine improvement of environmental health skills has become clearer as response strategies have been developed. The role of securing credible information is a continuing challenge at the local and national level as public, private, and community partners define their respective roles in addressing the medical, scientific, political, and economic dimensions of health promotion, prevention, treatment, remediation, and equity in service delivery.

Accountability and Strategic Collaboration

The RC National Advisory Board (NAB), which includes the project's community representatives, scientists, and health providers, offers a mechanism for accountability among the partnerships. NAB also provides a network for communities and scientists to locate each other and ascertain if a potential partnership is a match. NAB members also communicate regularly with each other and with RC staff.

The work of the Community-Responsive Partners Project has generated interest in institutions with the potential for wide-ranging impact on health policy. Following her involvement with the project, the Sumter County physician was elected to the Institute of Medicine (a subsidiary of the National Academy of Sciences) and appointed to its Environmental Justice Committee. Her work at EOHSI has also sparked interest in a regular residency program for community-based physicians in environmental health.

Collaborators at the El Paso model project made a presentation to the Environmental Justice Committee on the exposure of farmworkers to pesticides and made recommendations to the National Institute of Occupational Safety and Health on the research needs of farmworkers and their families.

Agriculture and Environmental Justice

A striking Year One outcome of the Binational Project on Pesticides was an unprecedented binational workshop organized by the Rural Coalition with support from NIEHS. Held at the Farmworker Center in El Paso, the meeting has led to new collaborative efforts among farmworkers, scientists, and government officials from both sides of the border. Participants proposed that a binational commission of farmworkers should be formed with the RC to study and monitor human rights violations, including pesticide poisoning, and to inform policymakers of the conditions which agricultural laborers face. Many disturbing facts were raised during the workshop: Over 4 million migrant farmworkers labor in the United States (Devers, 1991). Mexico's Ministry of Social Development reports that 3.6 million *jornaleros*, or farmworkers who do not own land, migrate within Mexico seeking work. These *jornaleros* "live below the minimum standards in health, education, and housing, despite the mandate from the Mexican Constitution," according to a spokesperson from the ministry. In the United States, farm work is one of the most hazardous occupations. Agricultural workers have an annual death rate five times greater than the national rate for all occupations combined (Devers, 1991). Researchers noted that only seven major studies on farmworkers and health had been completed (Fenske & Simcox, 1995).

Pesticides are linked to cancer, skin diseases, birth defects, sterility, and neurological problems. Pesticide exposure has resulted in over 300,000 cases of illness and over 1,000 deaths every year in the United States. Two Institute of Medicine representatives attending the workshop reported: "One of the telling points. . . came from the group that consisted solely of farmworkers. Their recommendations highlighted the concept that good science begins with asking the right question. . . . The farmworkers' comments demonstrated that their questions are not that different from those of scientists and underscored the value of lay input in defining the needs of the community with respect to research" (M. A. Smith, personal communication, July 9, 1996).

Generating New Partnerships and Sharing Results

Participants in both model projects are committed to share what has been learned with other Rural Coalition members and collaborators, and the coalition has begun to link other member groups to scientists and health providers. RC staff and board members facilitate development of collaborative partnerships, match communities with scientists, and enable community groups to learn how to work with scientific partners.

Four new collaborations were also initiated during the course of the four-year project, almost as many as were already in progress. The community in Columbia, Mississippi, site of the chemical plant explosion, is assembling a team to help respond to the community's concern about whether skin rashes, miscarriages, and other health problems are related to the explosion. Meetings and site visits have led to community collaboration proposals focusing on agricultural waste in North Carolina and "toxic donuts" of hazardous industries clustered in rural South Carolina.

To address the level of interest expressed elsewhere, new training for communities will become a regular part of the RC program. The coalition's experience in other states indicates that both race and poverty are key contributing factors to vulnerability to health risks. Initial findings indicate that health monitoring techniques are inadequate to address the needs of populations with combined risk factors. Some of these factors include multiple and severe exposure to hazards; compromised health status; and other economic and political conditions, such as company doctors or industry-funded research programs, which might have reason to understate problems. Because of these factors, instances of disease go unidentified or untreated due to lack of consistent and clear reporting on health outcomes as well as inadequate training of professionals in diagnosis and treatment.

Public initiative and support at the federal and state levels, university collaboration with community groups, and specialized training—including environmental health residencies—are among strategies with potential in these communities. Networks linking partners beyond the community are especially critical in producing credible evidence and effective strategies to help communities respond to very significant health care problems.

Applications to Professional Development

Health professionals can benefit from working in partnerships with communities to define and articulate health challenges and to develop appropriate skills and collaborative strategies for meeting community needs. Without adequate support, rural communities face health challenges that are beyond the capacity of even the most dedicated professionals. These challenges require a multidisciplinary collaborative approach and willingness form all partners to exercise leadership and speak honestly and coherently about political and economic issues. Recommended practices include community-responsive methods, multidisciplinary collaboration (which includes, at its very base, community-based organizations working with vulnerable populations), professional respect among diverse partners, competent design of research protocols (especially for use with high-risk populations whose exposures do not fit current research techniques), and routine basic training in environmental health. Technology can also play a supportive role if appropriate networks and training are developed and applied.

Of most concern to community-based members is the development of a well-informed and honest dialogue which joins all partners in a common voice to articulate problems and seek solutions that will restore health to rural communities and at-risk populations.

From the perspective of rural communities, this partnership model can address the effects of environmental factors on community, especially the effects of multiple toxic exposures. From the perspective of scientists, working with community groups poses challenges that can improve the process of collaboration and scientific research design. In addition, research geared to address problems of real concern to the community can elicit personal satisfaction. Finally, from the perspective of the health provider, such collaboration strengthens awareness of basic health service needs as well as of the special health needs of vulnerable communities.

The environmental health residency model, whereby a primary care physician builds contacts and clinical skills to recognize and treat environmentally and occupationally derived illnesses, was highly successful in the view of both communities and participating environmental centers. Replicating this program on a wide scale should be considered, as should a better method for regular, ongoing interdisciplinary networking and training.

Low-income rural communities that most need access to health services are least likely to have a health provider. For example, less than 20% of the population of migrant workers are served by migrant clinics. Even when migrant farmworkers have access to clinics, exposures to pesticides often go unrecognized. Health providers need to be recruited, familiarized, motivated, and trained to work with these populations in a proactive way commensurate with their dignity and needs.

An interdisciplinary board such as the RC National Advisory Board assures accountability for both scientists and communities, while at the same time it provides a forum for communities and scientists to get to know each other and assess if they are a "match."

Communities and health providers are learning from each other, and a mentoring process is occurring. Access to numerous scientific partners and community groups for potential "matches" continues to be an asset and speaks to the wisdom of constructing a broader project to enhance networking and collaboration in a broader set of communities and with a wider range of scientific research centers.

The NIEHS Environmental Justice Project grant represents a model that needs to be more broadly adapted among more well-funded public institutions and foundations. In addition, it is critical that rural environmental justice collaborations continue into RO1-type grants and projects and that community-responsive criteria be more widely applied. Agencies such as the National Cancer Institute and the Environmental Protection Agency could learn from community-responsive partners, and they could require outreach on behalf of NIEHS-funded research centers. All participants in these projects should use findings, evaluations, and contacts to promote community-responsive practices in research.

References

Devers, A. (1991). *Farmworkers and health.* Washington, DC: U.S. Department of Health and Human Services.

Fenske, R., & Simcox, N. (1995). Agricultural workers. In B. Levy & D. Wegman (Eds.), *Occupational health: Recognizing and preventing work-related disease.* Boston: Little Brown.

Marentes, C., et al. (1996, October). *Report on the Community-Responsive Partners for Environmental Health Project.* Presented to the National Institute of Environmental and Health Science, Environmental Justice Grantees meeting, Las Vegas, NV.

Robson, M. (1996, June). [Presentation to "Collaborative Partnerships with Farmworkers and Families: Pesticides, Agriculture and Environmental Justice on the U.S.-Mexico Border," Centro de Trabajadores Agricolas Fronterizos in El Paso, TX.]

7

Applying the Community-Responsive Model: New York State

Dwight C. Williams

For the past few years, as the Chief Health Planner, New York State Department of Health, I was responsible for developing plans, policies, and alternatives to maintain a health care presence in rural communities throughout New York. Being born and reared in Washington, DC, at first I wondered: Why me, and why rural health? But it took only a short while to realize that issues affecting health care in rural areas were very similar to those in urban areas. Regardless of geographic location, access to health care was and is still a common issue.

Whether people in community health focus on geographic access, by identifying barriers that make getting to one's health care provider a challenge; financial access, by working with people on their ability or inability to pay for care; or operational access, by concerning themselves with when providers are open for business—residents of rural and urban communities share all these concerns. We, professionals and residents alike, are all mindful that the health care we receive be affordable, coordinated, and of high quality. So, with this understanding, my place of birth really has little impact on an examination of rural health care issues.

Several years ago, I attended a national conference on rural health and learned about the hazards of working on farms and the health care risks farmers face. Acknowledging how dangerous farm work can be, the conference focused on the farmer and the need to preserve a health care presence in rural areas. However, today we are informed of the impact of farm work on farmworkers who may be immigrants and migrants and who frequently lack education and economic or political power.

For most of us, food growing and production are things we may take for granted—a trip to the supermarket to purchase our goods, back home to prepare them (if they aren't already), and finally we settle down to the dinner table. But how many of us have considered how, and under what circumstances, these products get to us? Have we considered the human side of this process? Who are these people, and what do they have to endure to make our lives more convenient and more comfortable? More specifically, what are the occupational hazards of the farmworker population?

In an environment of genetic engineering, mass production, and consumption, who advocates for the more than 8 million farmworkers in the United States and Mexico? Who is concerned about the impact that mass production and accelerated crop development has on this almost invisible work force? Specifically, who is concerned about the impact of pesticide poisoning and the associated risks these chemicals have on the health status of farmworkers?

Pesticides account for over 1,000 deaths and 300,000 cases of illnesses annually in the U.S.; they have been known to cause cancer, sterility, skin diseases, neurological problems, and birth defects. Although comparable data for Mexico are not available, we can speculate that the farmworking environment there poses the same or greater risks.

Using the Rural Coalition (RC) model, the answer to the aforementioned questions are social workers, practitioners, and scientists. In the previous chapter, Lorette Picciano demonstrated how a culturally diverse alliance of approximately 100 community-based members can facilitate bottom-up participation to increase society's awareness of the need for environmental justice. The RC has done this by securing grants to collaborate with universities, governments, and scientists to establish an agenda which places farmwork issues before policymakers.

The Community-Responsive Partners for Environmental Health is one such partnership, funded by the National Institute of Environmental Health Sciences to:

- empower rural communities to address issues related to work site protection;
- teach rural communities how to develop coalitions and collaborative strategies; and
- demonstrate that communities can identify and improve their health status outcomes by working with health care providers, scientists, and others.

The Rural Coalition model of community advocacy has facilitated the joining of scientists, researchers, the federal government, and poor and at-risk communities as partners defining issues and developing solutions. This in itself is significant; rarely are communities of this nature recognized as more than "study subjects" by scientific institutions.

The Sumter County Project (see Chapter 6) is teaching the community to share in the reporting of health problems that may be attributed to chemical dumping. Another effort, the Binational Pesticides Project of El Paso, Texas, has resulted in improved living conditions for migrant farmworkers.

The face of rural communities has changed. Residents of the aforementioned areas face declining job prospects and income. As a result, health benefits have decreased and access to a variety of services has also been severely reduced. The combination of these adversities increase the likelihood of exposure to environmental health hazards.

Quite often, when people think of the state of New York, New York City comes to mind. But of the 18 million persons residing in the state, 3.8 million live in rural areas. Of the 62 counties comprising the state, 44 (approximately 70%) are defined as rural.

Through my previous plan development and policy experiences, working with the Legislative Commission on Rural Resources and the Office of Rural Health, I have documented that, in 1986, there were 48 rural hospitals in New York state. By 1996, that number had dropped to approximately 30. With the assistance of these organizations, New York state has developed a policy to maintain a health care presence in rural areas.

In-state rural community residents have access to the Swing-Bed Demonstration Program, which allows rural hospitals to convert excess acute-care beds into short-term, nursing home rehabilitation beds. The Essential Access Community Hospital/Rural Primary Care Hospital program (EACH/RPCH) encourages smaller facilities to link with larger hospitals to increase access to health care, and the Rural Health Network has fostered the development of collaborative efforts to preserve a continuum of needed health services.

During my rural health care planning days, while identifying areas with low access to primary care, I once read an article in the *New York Times* that included a map of New York City's environmental dumps. The correlation between the low-access areas and the location of these dumps was shocking. These communities, although not rural, held some of the same distinctions: their inhabitants were mostly poor, under- or uneducated, minority, and seemingly powerless.

Health professionals, as noted by Dr. Picciano, can help at-risk rural communities through the formation of partnerships to identify environmental health hazards and by describing and recording changes in the community's health status. Assistance can also be provided in documenting effective treatment and preventive strategies and by informing the community of the social and political advantages of developing collaborative relationships with scientific and academic institutions.

Further, student internships that explore and practice the benefits of collaborative participation can be developed. Students can be prepared to identify and handle conflicting value systems, and universities can use actual case studies to develop superior practice models. Community leaders can be invited as guest lecturers to identify projects in need of assistance and further refinement. Such activities will add to the curriculum and foster practitioner advocacy.

It seems that, today, the need for advocacy has been replaced with a more conservative tone. We have replaced advocacy with terms like "personal responsibility and systems reform."

But there is a need for all of us, as social workers and helping professionals, to rethink advocacy and reemphasize the need for community, bottom–up involvement. This represents the real changing paradigm.

Part 3

Building on Strengths for Successful Collaboration and Partnerships

C ollaboration and partnerships are necessary ingredients for successful work between the university and the community, among different disciplines within the university, among different service providers in the community, and between helping professionals and their clients. Universities play a central role because they help students acquire the knowledge, skills, values, and abilities that allow them to be successful partners and bring about planned change. The chapters in this section provide theoretical and hands-on examples of the importance of working from a strengths perspective and how collaboration and partnerships between systems and between the university and the community can provide more comprehensive and effective services for children and families. These chapters reinforce the need for helping professionals to identify strengths within individuals and communities. They also emphasize that practitioners need to remember that they are not always the experts and can learn from those in need of services. Clients—whether individuals, families, or communities— have assets that should be mustered to help create change.

Partnerships and collaboration to enhance individual, family, and community well-being require several key ingredients that are outlined in the chapters in this section. They include:

- Ability to recognize and build on strengths;
- Ability to be culturally competent;
- Ability to develop shared goals and vision;
- Ability to share power;
- Ability to communicate across different languages, different communities, different professions, and different cultural norms;
- Ability to address social, economic, health, and educational needs of community members;
- Ability to let the community lead by allowing it to set goals and provide the value base.

The Strengths Perspective

The belief in people's capacity to transform themselves is deeply rooted in the social work tradition. Practitioners are encouraged to recognize the strengths within and around clients as building blocks of change. In Chapter 8, "The Strengths Perspective: Creating a Base for Social Work Practice," Ann Weick describes a practice framework for contemporary social work education based on the conviction that the person needing help brings a rich array of capacities, abilities, resources, and experiences that can support the process of change. Weick stresses that forming relationships lies at the core of successful social work practice. Although Weick's outline of the strengths perspective primarily addresses social work education and practice, her discussion of skills for good practice and implications for university education will speak to other helping professionals, who serve clients with multiple needs and strengths in an environment with multiple possibilities.

Community–University Partnerships

In her commentary on Weick's paper at the focus group meeting, Gloria Meert linked the strengths perspective to the assets-based approach taken by a Kellogg Foundation–funded 10-site initiative that focuses on families, neighborhoods, and communities. The initiative was designed to establish partnerships between higher education and community-based organizations to develop in-service and pre-service training that is more responsive to the complexities of family and neighborhood issues.

These community–university partnerships stress a "bottom up—top down" approach, where each member participates in the change process. Community members serve on advisory or steering committees with an equal voice in decision making; they also develop and deliver training modules for those interested in strengthening families and neighborhoods. In turn, the university brings expertise and resources to assist the community with training and other areas needing change. It also provides community members access to educational opportunities through fellowships or stipends. Together, the university and community make a concerted effort to address policy issues affecting families and the places where they live.

The assets-based approach has been promoted by John Kretzman and John L. McKnight of the Asset-Based Community Development Institute at Northwestern University. This approach serves as a framework for many current initiatives that focus on identifying and building on community strengths. These initiatives rely on a community capacity model, rather than a deficit/dysfunctional paradigm, and work with the knowledge that, even in the poorest communities, one can find assets in a variety of places: from residents' skills and talents to schools, libraries, churches, and so on.

Meert offered several questions to consider as organizations and institutions move toward working collaboratively with communities: What does a healthy community look like? What needs to happen to achieve a healthy community? What strengths and resources do members bring to the partnership? What are the members' commonalities and differences? Is there a consensus on the mission? How can power be shared if one member of the partnership is more dominant than the other?

These descriptions of the strengths perspective and assets-based community building highlighted the need for helping professionals to develop good relationships with the community. Community workers and academics need to go to the community and have residents define the community's unique traits. This requires good listening skills and respect for those who are different. Work with communities and individuals is highly individualized. Often, the most powerful work in a community happens at the informal level. Interaction is crucial—community workers should ask questions, rather than base their perceptions on their own cultural background. Diversity training, too, is crucial, and norma-tive assumptions about clients should not be encouraged.

From the university's standpoint, it is important to remember that students can make a positive impact on community change. Universities teach students values and skills. Students then take these values and skills to internship agencies and serve as agents of change, bringing their learning and experiences back to the university.

Building Community and Individual Self-Sufficiency

Patricia McDonald's chapter, "The Social Worker as Economic Information Entrepreneur: A New Paradigm for the 21st Century," provides a powerful case example from her work as a social work student at SUNYA. She describes how focusing on the strengths of the client and asserting the social worker's role as "information entrepreneur" can facilitate community economic development and individual economic self-sufficiency. McDonald describes her successful collaboration with a client who was receiving public assistance. A microenterprise was created that helped move the client and some acquaintances off welfare. McDonald demon-strates how the creation of microenterprises can provide valuable resources in rural U.S. communities. In the role of economic information entrepreneur, she suggests, the social worker must be able to wear many hats, including brainstormer, coordinator, teacher, networker, visionary, and healer.

Gloria Reynolds's response to McDonald's case study reiterates the many roles that helping professionals in rural communities must play. She suggests that professionals in rural communities are agents of change who need to partner with the community and who cannot succeed if they perceive themselves to be intellectual elitists. Reynolds also asserts the need for "intersectoral" coopera-tion between local businesses, religious organizations, civic groups, schools, political leaders, active citizens, and development organi-zations. Localities need to establish common goals, rather than rely on the central and intermediate levels of government to define needs and values. Instead, she says, higher levels of government can serve as facilitators that help localities meet their goals.

Collaboration and Partnerships across Cultures

Nurse, midwife, and educator Katsi Cook reinforces the importance of collaborative work with the community in Chapter 11, "Akwesasne Women: Meeting the Challenge of Environmental Threats." Such work should draw on community strengths and ensure the existence of clear communication. Her experiences in Native American communities show that conflicts arise between them and other communities because of differences in language, laws, and customs. For example, a New York state law making it unlawful to practice midwifery outside of a hospital can be a barrier to Indian childbirth practices. Nurses or midwifes who come to the village and assist in home births risk losing their licenses, and Cook asserts that it should be the woman's choice to have a traditional Akwesasne birth in her home.

Helping professionals coming into a Native American community often experience difficulty because of differences in language. The challenge is to build a relationship based on respect, equity, and empowerment to bridge the gap across such differences. Social workers should recognize that different cultures and communities communicate differently and that we have to learn to understand one another and how each of us communicates our feelings, biases, and barriers.

Cook describes how personal and community life go through cycles, and how individuals and communities struggle to cope and survive throughout changes. "All change begins as conflict and moves forward as a team," Cook says, turning to an example of the Akwesasne Indian village response to environmental hazards in upstate New York.

At the focus group meeting, Cook took participants on a guided journey to make her points more vivid. After asking the group's permission, she sang a traditional prayer song in her native tongue and guided the participants through a meditation. It served as a powerful reminder that when helping others we need to understand who they are and what beliefs and values guide their sense of well-being. It also reinforces the need to be open to new ways of learning and recognize that there are many ways of knowing.

Making Collaboration and Partnerships Work

In "Collaboration on Behalf of Individuals and Families in Rural Areas: Integrative, Community-based Strategies for Employment, Economic Development, and Well-Being," Katharine Briar-Lawson and Hal Lawson provide a historical perspective on how collaborative efforts on behalf of individuals, families, and communities have developed over the past decade. They assert the need for a stronger connection between current efforts to integrate social, educational, and health services for children and families and economic and community development strategies. These community-based initiatives also encourage the development of university-based cross-disciplinary endeavors. Diverse disciplines such as architecture, nursing, public administration, social work, education, law, and recreation might develop common curriculum areas covering, for example, empowerment, cultural competence, family-centered practice, economic development, income supports, occupational development, and job creation. This provides an opportunity for community leaders and their local collaboratives to join with university faculty and students, enriching the learning and change process for all. Collaboration is not an end in itself, Briar-Lawson and Lawson caution, but a means to improve individual, family, and community well-being.

They also stress the special needs of contemporary rural communities as they face a deteriorating economic environment and as repercussions of welfare reform continue to saddle women and children with limited access to jobs, child care, and transportation. Briar-Lawson and Lawson suggest that rural communities and their partners adapt to change and conflict by embarking on community capacity-building efforts. Solutions should be the focus, rather than blame for what does not exist, and as an example they suggest a barter system that could be arranged where families assist each other by "trading strengths" when the economic base cannot support a critical mass of money and jobs.

Consumer-guided collaborative practices require a balance between professional specialists, community residents, and para-professionals, as well as a shared foundation for practice across all who work in the community. Briar-Lawson and Lawson also describe how strategies for economically relevant, family-centered change need to include rural economic and community development, local and self-help strategies, social action strategies, and social planning.

In her response to Briar-Lawson's original presentation on collaboration and partnerships at the focus group meeting, Joan Sinclair emphasized the importance of collaboration in creating economic development programs that help current and former rural welfare recipients move toward economic self-sufficiency. In figuring out the right balance of state and federal aid for welfare recipients, the role of local community collaborators needs to be clearer. Sinclair described how local nursing homes are collaborating with the Allegany County (NY) Department of Social Services to train welfare recipients as aides in their facilities. Such public–private partnerships are imperative for economic success and social well-being, she said; businesses need to partner with the public sector to create positive community change. SUNYA graduate students James Izzo and Marissa Panton also suggested that involving the business world can help expand the collaborative vision. They noted that individuals with MBAs are skilled at assessing broad systems and possess skills in teamwork, collaboration, and leadership technology that can be shared with communities to strengthen coordination and collaboration. Persons with business training can be useful in helping a diverse group develop a common ground.

In the final chapter, "Interagency Collaboration and Coordination: Implications for Professional Development," Kathleen O'Brien describes how interagency collaboration and coordination can make a difference for homeless children. In addition to providing a helpful review of the literature on collaboration, interprofessional partnerships, and services to at-risk children and youth, O'Brien describes her research on interorganizational relationships between school districts and human service agencies that provide needed services. She found that communities with more effective interagency coordination had agencies working together to implement student service plans. Successful coordination among agencies often resulted in shared information, pooled resources, and joint funding of services or personnel, she says. Professional power was enhanced when agencies believed they mutually influenced each other. And effective working relationships focused less on specific professional expertise and more on interpersonal traits, such as the ability to work with others, develop trusting relationships, and follow through on commitments.

8

The Strengths Perspective: Creating a Base for Social Work Practice

Ann Weick

As the 20th century comes to a close, every venue of social living appears buffeted by the winds of change. In the social services, the dismantling of the welfare state, including its pillars of federal support, has set off tremors that will be felt in every community in America. The federal government's policy role is shifting to the states, and states have shifted much responsibility to the local level. The means by which this transfer is achieved, and the local structures that emerge to respond to new challenges, will determine both the shape of the social service delivery system and the fates of people needing services for many years into the future. These changes are occurring in the midst of the world in which social workers practice and thus present a matter for serious consideration.

Whenever large social change is underway, it is tempting to forecast its direction by looking at the past or the present. The signs of these times are not difficult to spot. Expectations that the federal government should maintain a minimum safety net for the most vulnerable members of society has eroded, replaced by suspicion of governmental authority and cynicism about the political process. Skyrocketing health care costs have led not to reform of the system but to attempts to cap expenditures, and managed care strategies in medical settings are now being adapted to mental health and child welfare. The notion that social stability requires means for redistributing resources has fallen out of favor as the gap between rich and poor has grown to its widest point in over 50 years. And consequences of growing violence, lack of opportunities for productive work, and racial and ethnic divisions create a sense of threat that is not easily dismissed. There seems to be little in these signs that would be useful for shaping a constructive, creative plan for the future.

Throughout its history, the profession has survived because it has been able to read the signs of the times. Although social work is deeply affected by the currents of social change, it has shown a capacity to develop creative responses and, in some circumstances, to provide leadership for new policy and service initiatives. Being able to lead in these uncertain times requires a critical examination of what the profession has contributed thus far, and a push to bring fresh understandings to some of its most deeply held wisdom. Such an assessment can serve to illuminate the role of social workers in today's society and throw light on the education necessary for meeting this challenge.

One pressing professional concern has been the lack of an articulate and compelling core of values, knowledge, and skills that underlie social work's commitment to helping vulnerable people. Social work consciously chose the position of being the profession in the middle, with the task of negotiating between the client and other systems (Shulman, 1992). Although social workers bring to this task an astounding array of skills, experience, and perspectives, society's general dismissal of the importance of this work contributes to an uneasy dilemma. What social workers know how to do best is undervalued and largely ignored, and their responses to this situation tend to fall in two directions: either quietly carry out one's work, knowing these contributions are uniquely important, or mimic the skills of other professions whose status appears more widely accepted and assured.

Social work's assessment of its own professional capacities is an important base from which to look toward the future. If we believe that our survival depends upon aligning more closely with professions such as medicine and nursing, or disciplines such as psychology and family therapy, because they appear to hold stronger positions in the changing environment of social and health services, then we are likely to become indistinguishable from them. The need for status and security will ultimately lead to our professional demise. If, on the other hand, we believe that the profession can make a unique contribution, then we must take on the serious challenge of reclaiming and reaffirming the knowledge, values, and skills that rest at our professional core.

Strengths at the Core

The belief in people's capacity to transform themselves is deeply rooted in social work tradition. Building on people's strengths has been an accepted, if largely unrecognized, practice maxim throughout our history. Early writers such as Mary Richmond (1917), Bertha Reynolds (1951), and Ruth Smalley (1967) exhorted practitioners to recognize and honor the strengths within and around clients as building blocks for change. The development of a fresh perspective on this long-held value provides a window through which to see how reclaiming our knowledge can help redirect social work practice and education for practice.

The strengths perspective has existed in its contemporary form for over 15 years. It began as an approach for helping people with severe and persistent mental illness. In the early 1980s at the University of Kansas School of Social Welfare, Professor Charlie Rapp and then-doctoral student Ronna Chamberlain began constructing a strategy for preparing MSW students to work in community mental health centers by turning the tables on the dominant pathology model. Instead of focusing on clients' diagnosed symptoms, they established a model of practice that gave singular attention to client strengths. This entailed concentrating on clients' particular talents and abilities, their history of past survival success, and their life aspirations. This orientation helped evolve a model of case management in which workers and clients formed a partnership to orchestrate personal, family, and community resources to meet client goals (Rapp & Chamberlain, 1985; Rapp & Wintersteen, 1989). As others have refined it, the model has been used to train thousands of social work, mental health, and other human service workers in over 40 states, in England, and in Australia. The model has also been successfully used for other vulnerable populations such as children with severe and persistent mental illness, women on welfare, the frail elderly, and persons on parole.

In the last decade, the model has been extended beyond case management to a more general practice orientation (Saleebey, 1992, 1996; Weick, Rapp, Sullivan, & Kisthardt, 1989). By creating a conscious focus on the strengths that people bring to the social work encounter, the ensuing work is dramatically reframed. The problem focus, which gained acclaim by way of psychological theory and through Perlman's (1963) problem-solving model, no longer receives the dominant attention. Problems are not ignored, but in the strengths perspective they do not occupy center stage (Weick & Chamberlain, 1996). Instead, the work begins with a conviction that the person needing help brings a rich array of capacities, abilities, resources, and experiences that can support the process of change.

The social work tradition represents a broad range of practice approaches. It draws on the rich history of social group work, which emphasizes the power inherent in mobilizing group resources. It uses the community-based approaches inherent in case management services for vulnerable populations. It builds on the experience of community organization and, more recently, community development efforts. It reflects a wide interest, too, in the development of social policy and systems of social service delivery. The strengths perspective is firmly ensconced among these wide views of practice.

Reorienting practice through a strengths perspective is only one avenue for excavating the deeper wisdom underlying social work knowledge. It serves as a model process with which the profession can reclaim its heritage, and illuminates processes that can be applied to other domains of social work knowledge and skills. Through the strengths perspective, something old can be made new. Social work professionals can retrieve a robust potential from what seems a disarmingly simple idea and, at the same time, articulate more clearly some of the most deeply held notions about human behavior and human change.

Learning from the Strengths Perspective

Ideas have the power to change our worldview, and typically such ideas run counter to prevailing wisdom. They bubble beneath the surface of conventional beliefs in a murky, unrecognized, and unutilized form. Such is the case of the strengths perspective. For all the years of its history, the profession retained allegiance to the maxim "Build on people's strengths." That it did so even when this was not the theoretical, or more recently financial, base for professional practice is a tribute to a strong, yet often unarticulated, value-based practice perspective. In many ways the strengths perspective is emblematic of the profession's value foundation. To pursue strengths-based practice, one must have an unswerving belief in people's capacity to grow and change; a deep respect for people's own judgments about what they need and how they want to live their lives; a willingness to collaborate with clients and thus share power; and a sophisticated set of skills to help people negotiate complex systems, garner needed information, and advocate for essential services. Such commitments activate the values embedded in good practice and give them more vital and recognizable forms.

The strengths perspective also contributes to the reclarification of social work knowledge. Practicing from a strengths perspective requires a different way of appraising legitimate knowledge. In a psychologically based practice model, knowledge derives from theory, and theory resides in the head of the practitioner by dint of professional education. Therefore, legitimate knowledge is the purview of the professional practitioner. In a strengths perspective, the definition of knowledge is radically expanded. Though professional knowledge is acknowledged and respected, practitioners also understand that multiple "knowledges" are present in a helping situation. Clients bring the most crucial kinds of knowledge: knowledge of the situation being confronted, with all of its difficulties, pain, challenges, and history; knowledge of life experiences and how they have survived thus far; and cultural and family knowledge reflected in stories, rituals, and myths. In traditional approaches, the legitimacy of these kinds of knowledge is largely discounted; the client's personal experience is seen as the material with which to sketch in the "real" story, seen through the theoretical lens of the practitioner and embellished by diagnosis or other psychological assessment.

Taking a strengths-based approach radically expands the boundaries of legitimate knowledge. By attending to peoples' knowledge of their lived experience and by actively soliciting their hopes and dreams for a more satisfying life, social workers become allies who use their professional knowledge and experience to help bring about desired changes. Giving a legitimate place to clients' own experience redefines the nature of knowledge (Weick, 1990). Rather than basing professional work on the social worker's knowledge, the strengths perspective assumes that constructive work will take place only when clients are recognized as experts about their own lives.

Explicit sharing and validation of different and legitimate forms of knowledge implicitly redefines the nature of the professional relationship. In conventional, psychologically based practice, the person needing help is typically viewed as less knowledgeable and less capable of change than the professional worker. Thus, the worker is in control of the situation and responsible for orchestrating the proper sequence of interactions. With this responsibility comes the power to define the person's situation and mental state, to determine access to needed resources, and to create the conditions for receiving help. In contrast, practice from a strengths perspective recognizes the legitimacy and necessity of fully incorporating the person's own knowledge about his or her life. The work begins as a conscious partnership in which each party has an important yet distinct contribution to make to the process.

To carry out such a partnership, the social worker's skills require a new level of conscious articulation. The strengths perspective accentuates these skills and, in doing so, helps highlight the contributions that professional social work makes within the social service arena. The necessary self-consciousness with which these skills must be described shows again the profession's constant challenge to explain itself and its work to the broader society. Thus, the question "What is it about social work that is different from other helping professions?" becomes more specific: "How can the strengths perspective highlight these essential differences?"

Strengths-based practice requires social workers to seriously revise and revalue what they know and what they think they know. For over 50 years social workers have thought they know best why people develop the problems they do. In a variety of forms, generations of social workers have been educated unwittingly on a two-track curriculum stream. On one level, they have learned to be social workers by being exposed to the broad context of social services and social policy and to the history and values of the profession. On another level, they have learned theories of human behavior, scientifically based approaches to research, and practice skills that derive from a worldview at odds with, if not in direct opposition to, the deepest values of the profession.

Because the strengths perspective does not treat problems or symptoms as the main focus, the knowledge that many social workers might most comfortably claim is no longer needed. Again, it is not that the problems people bring are insignificant or irrelevant. On the contrary, the problem receives attention because it begins the work where the client is. The strengths perspective asserts that focusing on the problem will not lead in a constructive or goal-satisfying direction. In those situations where the problem is acute and presents some form of harm to the client or to others, a clearly delineated response strategy needs to be developed (Weick & Chamberlain, 1996). However, the ongoing relationship forms around a recognition process in which the client and worker begin slowly noticing, identifying, and affirming the client's abilities, capacities, and aspirations for change. As the client begins to recognize goals for action, no matter how small, the social worker uses acquired knowledge to give this direction shape and substance.

The focus of strengths perspective work is also not on the past or present, but the future. The past and the present can be useful as a lesson book. From their experiences, clients can learn how to survive, what worked, what did not, and what aspects of themselves were strengthened and made more accessible for conscious use. This orients practice toward the future: given the current situation, how would clients like their situation to change? The social worker helps move from the guilt and pain of the past to the promise of the future. Recognizing that the social worker needs to help the client move into the future is one of the hidden skills of social work that forms the core of good practice.

The Skills of Good Practice

As much as social workers talk about skills, it would seem an easy task to outline what they are. Clearly, every good social worker has learned them, sometimes almost subliminally, and uses them every day. However, the profession's ability to write about them and social workers' ability to describe them are limited by two connected reasons: social work skills are neither theoretically appealing nor widely valued. The skills that account for social work's real value in society arc the plain but sophisticated skills that the strengths perspective brings to the forefront because, like the perspective itself, they are action skills. Conventional psychological practice models are strongly tilted toward talk. Talking about one's problems in sophisticated detail is seen as a sign of progress. In contrast, strengths-oriented skills are directed toward actions that help a person, family, or community identify and accomplish changes in its situation.

Thcse action skills are both well known and undervalued. They appear modcst and simple, without thc professional gloss of psychological approaches. And while complete development of this skill base involves extensive details, the general approach is sufficient to begin outlining some of its features.

Social work skills begin with the complex art of forming a relationship, harkening back to the very early social work concept of the relationship as the medium of change. The ability to establish a positive relationship, even in adverse circumstances, is a feat that social workers perform many times each day. It rests on an artistic orchestration of a rich array of values and knowledge that are brought to the interactive moment. The work is client-focused and is based on the belief that people must be actively involved in processes affecting their lives.

As the relationship develops, social workers tap into a knowledge base that is dramatically shaped by the profession's holistic perspective. Unlike in other professions, people are considered in their multiple social, physical, political, and cultural environments. A good social work practitioner assesses all aspects within and around the person, family, or community as elements of the change process, and also relies on clients' own accounting of these elements. Social workers' skill in systems assessment places them in the enviable role of "big picture" experts who are able to work with and influence complex systems.

The ability to locate, coordinate, and create needed resources represents another skill area of incalculable value to social workers. It is one thing to listen well to what people need; it is another to help them get it. Social workers need to be masters at orchestrating resources. They must work to develop a complex information and referral network that creates lines of communication across the entire community. The skills of relationship building, negotiation, and task focus all support this important area of work.

Though discrete and identifiable, these skill areas cumulatively create what might be called *human process skills*. These are not by-products of social work—these *are* social work. Whether in direct or indirect practice, social workers are connecting, communicating, advocating, assessing, facilitating, mediating, supporting, and collaborating. It is time to reclaim this distinctive role as process experts.

Education for Practice

If the strengths perspective presents avenues for renewing the profession's position as a vital partner in addressing our challenging times, then many of its contributions will change the shape of social work education. A first step toward change begins with a conscious critique of the profession's reliance on psychologically based theories of human behavior and change. With the exception of developments in resilience theory (Haggerty, Sherrod, Garmezy, & Rutter, 1994), generations of students have learned a pastiche of personality and human development theories that center on the problems, shortcomings, and limitations of humankind. Unfortunately, these theories are rarely taught from a critical perspective, where their assumptions are exposed and their implications for practice consciously analyzed. Instead, students are often left to create their own framework for practice.

The process of making social work's conceptual ground more consistent with our proclaimed practice sensibilities will form a major part of the backdrop for developing skills that lie at the heart of practice. Foundation courses in policy and social welfare history can continue to shape the larger social context for practice. Teaching practice skills from a strengths perspective encourages educators and students alike to reflect on approaches to practice curricula, and it frames them with values that have underwritten social work from its beginnings.

By reorienting education for practice, social work students, educators, and practitioners are better able to respond to the need for a more conscious articulation of core knowledge and skills. They need to communicate these within the profession itself and to the broader society. The issue is not whether social workers have the requisite knowledge and skills—they do. Nor is the issue whether society needs these skills—it does. However, skills learned in the absence of a clear philosophical framework prepare students to be adequate technicians but inept professional social workers. The strengths perspective infuses a value structure that informs both knowledge and skills and helps ensure that the artistic and pragmatic aspects of helping are fully present.

The process of rediscovering and reclaiming is very much at the heart of the strengths perspective. The issue is not whether people have the assets, experience, and capacities to transform their lives, but whether people can be helped to recognize and discover these strengths and then harness them in the service of their goals and aspirations. The process of reclamation is, at its essence, an empowerment process.

How fitting it would be, then, for social work to apply to itself its own best practice. Just as an individual or family or community can enjoy a renewed sense of power when its own resources are activated, so can the profession be renewed when its deepest knowledge is validated and given voice. If social work allows its own knowledge to revolutionize its professional self-conception, it will set in motion a power that can radiate outward to all areas of the professional setting. In doing so, it sets an example from its own process: that recognizing one's strengths is a felicitous base from which to engage in transformative practice.

Summary

Dramatic changes in the delivery of social services pose new and unsolved challenges to social work education and practice. One response to this state of affairs is to be adaptive; the other to be assertive. The latter response is the desirable one. These times require the profession to frame itself in the context of its own history and practice so that it will be able to lead, rather than follow.

The strengths perspective offers a means to critically reexamine and reclaim the knowledge, skills, and values that provide the profession with some of its deepest wisdom. In contrast to problem-focused psychological practice approaches, the strengths perspective requires the conscious employment of basic social work values, the reconstruction of legitimate knowledge, and the re-identification of social work skills. Included in this examination is a renewed appreciation for social work's position in collaborative ventures and a refurbished understanding of the common base of social work practice.

These arenas form the foundation for a different view of the nature of practice and of education for practice. In spite of strong currents that have drawn social work into more individually focused practice theories, the social work tradition resonates with a broader perspective on practice. Social group work, case management services, community organization and development, social policy, and service delivery systems all reflect an expansive view of social work practice. What is now needed is further explication of the knowledge and skills that infuse this work, and more strategies to reestablish social work's valid position as the "big picture" experts.

Moving away from a pathology perspective is a first step in reclaiming the broader world of possibilities inherent in strengths-based approaches to human change. From the individual and family to the community and its institutions, practice from a strengths perspective permits a seamless strategy of activating human, social, and physical resources in service of transformative goals. By relying on this perspective, the challenges facing the social work profession can appear more malleable and more responsive to innovative human actions. In fact, we might discover, as the strengths perspective proclaims, that we have always had the resources within and around us to fashion a more just and caring social context for all.

References

Haggerty, R. J., Sherrod, L. R., Garmezy, N., & Rutter, M. (1994). *Stress, risk, and resilience in children and adolescents: Processes, mechanisms and interventions*. Cambridge, England: Cambridge University Press.

Perlman, H. H. (1963). *Social casework: A problem solving process*. Chicago: University of Chicago Press.

Rapp, C. A., & Chamberlain, R. (1985). Case management services to the chronically mentally ill. *Social Work, 30*(5), 412-422.

Rapp, C. A., & Wintersteen, R. (1989). The strengths model of case management: Results from twelve demonstrations. *Psychosocial Rehabilitation Journal, 13*(1), 23-32.

Reynolds, B. (1951). *Social work and social living.* New York: Citadel.

Richmond, M. (1917). *Social diagnosis.* New York: Russell Sage Foundation.

Saleebey, D. (Ed.). (1992). *The strengths perspective in social work practice.* White Plains, NY: Longman.

Saleebey, D., (Ed.). (1996). *The strengths perspective in social work practice* (2nd ed.). White Plains, NY: Longman.

Shulman, L. (1992). *The skills of helping* (3rd ed.). Itasca, IL: F.E. Peacock.

Smalley, R. E. (1967). *Theory for social work practice.* New York: Columbia University Press.

Weick, A. (1990). Knowledge as experience: Exploring new dimensions of social work inquiry. *Social Thought, 16*(3), 36-46.

Weick, A., & Chamberlain, R. (1996). The place of problems in the strengths perspective. In D. Saleebey (Ed.), *The strengths perspective in social work practice* (2nd ed.). White Plains, NY: Longman.

Weick, A., Rapp, C., Sullivan, W. P., & Kisthardt, W. (1989). A strengths perspective for social work practice. *Social Work, 34*, 350-354.

9

The Social Worker as Economic Information Entrepreneur: A New Paradigm for the 21st Century

Patricia McDonald

As Toffler (1970), Naisbitt (1990), and others have predicted, the industrial age has given way to the age of information, and the effects of this change in mindset reach all professions in society, especially social work. This chapter describes a future role for social workers as *economic information entrepreneurs*, focusing on the contributions this new dimension to practice can make to rural communities. According to Andersen and Dawes (1993), an "Information Entrepreneur" in a rural system would use knowledge of the local community and its capabilities to package solutions for client problems. A social worker in this context could provide services, particularly those of an economic nature, to rural families at risk. Thus, the economic information entrepreneur I envision would be a creative messenger of change who educates for economic empowerment through economic literacy.[1]

Problem Formulation and Assessment

During my field placement last year in rural Schoharie County, New York, I visited a client who had just left her abusive husband after 25 years of marriage and needed help starting a new life. The woman was feeling quite hopeless and depressed about getting off

---

[1] Thanks to Joan Sinclair for planting the seed of this idea in a lecture she gave to the macro practice class at SUNYA on microenterprise as a pathway from poverty in rural environments.

public assistance and finding a job. She did not drive, had minimal work experience, and was diagnosed as clinically depressed. To make matters worse, her hometown was in the middle of a downward spiral toward economic depression. A large discount chain had opened a distribution center down the road and a new store in a town 10 miles away, thus forcing the closing of smaller stores in town. Exacerbating this problem was the seasonal economy of the town, which boomed as a health resort in the summer for Orthodox Jews from New York City and remained a virtual ghost town from September to June. This left an economically and socially fragmented community with limited opportunities and resources.

Intervention

Upon assessing my client's strengths, I found she experienced some success as a bank teller and was comfortable with bookkeeping and numbers. Her social network consisted of one best friend, with whom she had a dream to start an adult education center that would bring together a community depressed on many levels and could provide jobs for themselves and others. They found a vacant commercial building with very low rent and were highly motivated, but they lacked start-up capital or knowledge about creating a small business. This need gave birth to my role as economic information entrepreneur, and I decided that by helping my client and her friend create this business as a microenterprise, many of my client's problems could be solved and many community problems could be addressed.

Planning and Goals Formulation

Borrowing from cognitive theory (Beck, 1976) and creativity theory (Fritz, 1984), I had my client and her friend develop their vision for the adult learning center by writing down concrete ideas as they were formulated. Their homework was to expand upon these ideas in a daily journal, written at a designated time every morning. This technique, called "morning papers" (Cameron, 1992), maintained the momentum of their creativity as their ideas flowed freely and powerfully. They decided to call their enterprise The Creative Learning Center and came up with ideas for courses based on the skills and talents of the people they knew in the community. If created, it would be an excellent exercise of collaboration and coordination of community resources. There would be courses in holistic healing; planting herb gardens; landscape painting; interior decorating; and country banjo, guitar, violin, and mandolin lessons. In addition, courses were planned in home brewing, basic electricity, computer literacy, auto mechanics, carpentry, quilt making, gourmet cooking, and job-finding and job-keeping skills for adults and teenagers. Drawing on her best bank teller skills, my client would be the bookkeeper and business manager. Her friend would be the entrepreneur/idea person. We found free technical assistance from the SUNY–Cobleskill Office for Small Business Development, and I provided social skills training for public relations and community canvassing.

We developed a needs assessment with a roster of classes and space for suggestions. Prospective students and teachers were asked to circle the top three classes they would like to take and to write in classes they would like to teach. Proposals for microenterprise seed grants were written, and bank loans were sought. While waiting for a response, my client and her friend decided to seek donations, but they found it was illegal to take donations without a nonprofit license. Upon further investigation, we learned that such a license cost $500.

Back at the "drawing board" and holding firmly to this vision, my client and her friend generated the idea of starting a consignment shop to raise capital. It would be housed on the ground floor of their building and would be named "Diamonds and Rust." The shop would become an advertisement for the future center, and future teachers would sell their wares. Artists could sell their work, dressmakers their clothes, cooks their culinary creations, and poets their poetry; auto mechanics and electricians could sell their services. The producers/teachers would benefit, and my microentrepreneurs could eventually buy their nonprofit license and pay the rent with a percentage of the sales. Eventually, they planned, students could learn to make these products at the new center.

Both the consignment shop and the adult education center are exercises in economic collaboration and coordination, partnership and teamwork, where everyone from client to family to institution to community wins (Covey, 1990). Such vision and ideas stimulate economic development, create partnerships and resources, draw on communal strengths, and enable healthy economic, political, educational, and psychological growth. I tracked the women's progress using Kettner's (1985) change model. At the time of the focus group meeting, they had reached Stage 5, resource planning, and were intending to open the shop in May 1996.

Generating Resources

What was lacking in our grand scheme of creativity and collabo-ration was technical assistance. SUNY–Cobleskill was helpful to a certain extent, but I felt it would be useful to investigate other microenterprise projects that could provide support and the wis-dom of experience. I thought a microenterprise advisory network, perhaps with an interactive satellite video session, might fill this need, and so set out on a search for 'microenterprise advisors.' Joan Sinclair at the Allegany County (NY) Department of Social Services (DSS) directed me to Patti Croop at an "economic watchdog" organization in Albany called SENSES (Statewide Emergency Net-work for Social and Economic Security). This network of major human service, religious, and labor organizations in New York state has, among other accomplishments, a statewide community eco-nomic development network that organizes statewide and regional meetings and training sessions. SENSES assists network members in developing and carrying out a public policy agenda, and a particu-lar focus has been on overcoming the barriers that public assistance recipients face in starting their own businesses, creating jobs, and obtaining core funding for community economic development ventures.

SENSES provided me with excellent resource information. I found the Minority and Women Micro Enterprise Loan Fund (aka., The Micro Program), which enables corporations to make loans of up to $7,000 to minority- and women-owned microenterprises with no more than $100,000 in annual gross revenues. Loan funds can be used for such items as working capital, acquisition of machinery and equipment, and revolving lines of credit. This program could have filled the gap for my client and friend since they had no seed money. In addition, the Empire State Development Corporation funded three nonprofit businesses in 1995, providing each with $25,000 loans. Another possibility would be the Employee Owner-ship Project of the Albany Region (EOP), a nonprofit corporation designed for the purpose of fostering the creation, maintenance, and growth of enterprises that employ and are owned by low-income residents of the Albany area. EOP accomplishes this by offering intensive levels of assistance to a small number of enter-prise developers. The organization has assisted in the formation of nearly two dozen enterprises, creating over 45 full-time jobs for low-income people, many of whom were receiving public assistance.

A fourth advisory source was the Worker Ownership Resource Center (WORC), a community economic- and business-development organization dedicated to empowering low-income and other disadvantaged people to participate more fully in their local economies through creation of business enterprises. WORC assists its target population with comprehensive training programs that include one-on-one consultations, intensive classroom training workshops, technical assistance for completing business plans, access to small loans, peer support groups, mentoring programs, and monthly business workshops. WORC grew out of an effort by local activists to promote worker-owned, cooperatively managed enterprises. In 1992, it changed its focus toward community and microenterprise development. WORC is chartered to operate in 10 counties of south-central New York state. They have completed 15 microenterprise training programs, helping to start or expand more than 50 businesses. At the time of the focus group meeting, they had made 15 micro loans in the amount of $62,000.

Two successful businesses spawned by WORC are the Alfredia White Day Care Center and the Tangela Clark Hair Salon. White was already caring for children out of her home when she used WORC's training sessions and one-on-one technical assistance to start her business and apply for a loan. With her loan she purchased a van with which she could do activities with the children. In two years she has achieved financial independence and paid off her loan. Tangela Clark's hair salon specializes in the care and styling of African-American hair. WORC enabled her to expand her business from a booth she was renting at a local hair salon. After completing her training and a technical assistance program, she received a $3,000 loan to rent an additional booth and to purchase new equipment and a start-up inventory of products. Tangela continues to be involved in WORC's alumni network and receives ongoing support from WORC staff. WORC's alumni network would be a valuable resource for beginning microentrepreneurs in need of support and technical assistance.

The ACCORD Corporation, located in upstate New York's rural Allegany County, is a community action agency that works to help public assistance recipients locate and hold jobs. In 1987, it sponsored the Small Business Development Program (SBPD), which has been actively involved in the development of strategies to help self-employed public assistance recipients become self-sufficient business operators. Through funding from the U.S. Department of Housing and Urban Development's Microenterprise Program and the New York State Department of Economic Development's Entrepreneurial Assistance Program (EAP), ACCORD continues to provide training to this specialized clientele. The organization is part of the Allegany County "One Stop" employment and training program. Through these efforts, ACCORD has sponsored JOB TRACK, the county's name for its workforce efforts (Croop, Hennessy, & Ferraro, 1996).

The Allegany county–based EAP is a microenterprise program that benefits minorities, women, and dislocated workers in economically distressed areas. It uses a systematic approach to business creation, management, and expansion, and works on local and regional community economic development strategies. EAP's focus on start-ups and microenterprises owned by minorities and women distinguishes it from the state's other business assistance programs.

Another productive result of persistent networking was the discovery of Peter Glassman, director of the Albany-based Entrepreneurial Opportunity Program. He directed me to "Choices," a consignment shop in rural Ravena, NY. In a telephone interview, owner Linda Bruno said she was able to start her business with a small grant from the Albany County DSS. Her county legislator found out about it and brought her to the attention of a local state senator who helped her with additional funding. My client and her friend soon began networking with her for technical assistance. Such networking is crucial for start-up businesses, as evaluations of the ACCORD SBPD conclude:

> By their very nature, community action agencies have relied on extensive networking both in obtaining financial resources and in delivering programs. Networking skills have been an important ingredient in the business development activity of most enterprises involved in the SBDP. SBDP staff have initiated network contacts and they have consciously sought to develop networking skills among SBDP participants. (Szcerbacki, 1988)

As an economic information entrepreneur, I would organize Bruno and other microenterprise entrepreneurs around the state to create a 'Microenterprise Advisory Network.' Through the "People's Network," which broadcasts training seminars to corporations via satellite and is working on a network of grassroots entrepreneurs (M. Melia, unpublished interview, March 28, 1996), I would ask for donations of satellite dishes. The idea would be for my client and her friend, along with Bruno and others, to share their stories on video about how they got started, how they dealt with trials and tribulations, etc., thus providing technical assistance and motivational training. I pictured this growing into a statewide network, and then maybe beyond—a good use of technology as a vehicle for change, for the improvement of community economic development.

Treasury secretary Robert Rubin endorses the idea of empowering economically disadvantaged people through microenterprise, calling his idea "trickle-up economics" (Weisberg, 1996). This idea came to him when he was in the Philippines visiting the Most Holy Redeemer Multipurpose Cooperative in a poor section of Manila. He spoke with a woman there who had taken advantage of the church-sponsored microenterprise lending project to open a small restaurant, underwritten by the Asian Development Bank. Rubin was very impressed, saying, "I wish that every member of Congress could see a project like this, particularly those that believe in a capitalist system. . . because what is this? This is really dealing with the problems of poverty through capitalism, through enabling the poor to become part of the economy, enabling them to become part of the private sector" (Weisberg, 1996, pp. 32–37). Rubin believes that 'micro-lending'—helping less-than-credit-worthy cottage enterprises borrow at market rates—can be applied to areas where lack of funds prevents small businesses from getting off the ground.

Conclusion

As economic information entrepreneur, social workers must be willing to wear many hats: those of a brainstormer, coordinator, collaborator, teacher, networker, visionary, and healer. Following Kahn's (1969) holographic model, they must be able to channel other forces and resources in the community. They must be able to tap into the strengths of the client and the community and to enable a synergy of talent and vision for rural economic development. They must have the courage and commitment to go to the sources of political and economic power (Haynes & Mickelson, 1991). By touring the many projects described in this chapter—or someday watching a microenterprise advisory network on satellite video—Congress could witness these pioneers in a system of "trickle-up economics." Providing information from the frontlines for microenterprise and community empowerment: It feels like an idea whose time has come.

References

Andersen, D. F., & Dawes, S. (1993). Information entrepreneurs: The missing link in providing services to rural families at risk. In S. Jones (Ed.), *Sociocultural and service issues in working with rural clients* (pp. 245-253). Albany, NY: Rockefeller College Press.

Beck, A. T. (1976). *Cognitive therapy and emotional disorders.* New York: International University Press.

Cameron, J. (1992). *The artist's way.* New York: Tarcher/Perigree.

Covey, S. (1990). *The seven habits of highly effective people.* New York: Simon and Schuster.

Croop, P., Hennesy, K., & Ferraro, R. (1996–97). *Counterbudget.* Albany, NY: SENSES.

Fritz, R. (1984). *The path of least resistance.* Salem, MA: DMA Press.

Haynes, H., & Mickelson, J. (1991). *Affecting change: Social workers in the political arena.* New York: Longman.

Kahn, A. J. (1969). Theory and practice of social planning. New York: Russell Sage Foundation.

Kettner, P. (1985). *Initiating change in organizations and communities.* Belmont, CA: Wadsworth.

Naisbitt, J. (1990). *Megatrends 2000.* New York: Avon.

Szcerbacki, D. (1988). *Evaluation of the Small Business Development Program.* Produced for Allegany County Community Opportunities and Rural Development, New York.

Toffler, A. (1970). *Future shock.* New York: Bantam.

Weisberg, J. (1996, April 22). Clinton's best case. *New York,* pp. 32-37.

10

Response to "The Social Worker as Economic Information Entrepreneur: A New Paradigm for the 21st Century"

*Gloria J. Reynolds**

Helping and caring communities start with caring individuals. And as caring professionals we must be the fodder, fuel, and spark that starts the engine not only to a new vision but to a new way of interacting with the people we live closest to: our families, our neighbors, local businesses, local governments, and communities.

Pat McDonald has presented an idea whose time must come. Is that time now?

I believe so. A movement is underway, though hidden and not yet fully developed. By exchanging ideas and thoughts at this conference, we are participating in that movement toward civic cooperation and helping partnerships. Creative energy and vitality exist but need encouragement, openness, and technical and financial assistance.

Rural areas are isolated not just by their distance from city centers but by separation in cultures. Professionals in rural communities must act as agents for change, not as intellectual elitists but as partners with their community. Advocacy, or allowing the "trickle up" to happen, is part of this partnership; communication and information are also central to this upward movement.

There is an imbalance of information in the many sectors that affect and are affected by social work. But where is this asymmetry? Is the problem one of dissemination from above, or of poor reception from below? As agents of change, we have a responsibility to

* The author thanks Patricia McDonald for allowing her to read and critique her paper. She also thanks Diane Dewar and Carol Young for involving her in the focus group meeting.

listen to the values and needs of those around us, and only then can we truly be information entrepreneurs. The agency relationship is a direct consequence of the professional providers' informational advantage. Asymmetric information is an inevitable by-product of specialization; because professionals specialize, they know more about their own specialty than others. This is the norm, not the exception (Scitovsky, 1990). The agents' information advantage thus places a special responsibility on them to act in the client's best interest.

A social worker might know more about the larger world of information acquisition, but the client is more knowledgeable about his or her own needs and about the politics, culture, and social structure of the local community. Clients are our liaisons to a better understanding of their unique environment.

As evidenced in the previous chapter, Pat McDonald listened and then helped. She did not direct, dictate, stifle, or discourage, but assisted clients to become more successful, not only in business development but in personal development. She facilitated the client in meeting her goal of improved welfare by giving information related to business and educational opportunities.

As people become more integrated into their locality, they become more aware of available resources, whether from urban activity centers or federal levels. This greater involvement expands one's worldview and one's own sense of value to society. Through the social worker's intervention, clients become more empowered, and their contributions can result in improved community welfare. (I say *can* because when discussing microeconomics and new business ventures, the clients are the ultimate entrepreneurs. They take the economic risk when assuming a loan, making commitments, and signing lease agreements.)

Social workers are closely involved with individuals, a fact made evident in McDonald's paper by the assistance given to the individual decision maker. The more information that can be given to the individual decision maker, the more competitive the economy becomes. This leads to more symmetry, or a better balance between urban versus rural, large versus small, powerful versus less powerful, wealthy versus those with fewer resources.

Satellite dish technology can bring relevant information into homes and businesses, no matter where they are located. As technology becomes less expensive and as information and financial assistance are available, small businesses and communities can have access not only to urban and university centers but to international innovations.

But let us not forget our responsibility to the macro economic view. Changing the "trickle down" movement to a "trickle up" movement requires that the present system be turned upside down. As agents for the small, the rural, the less endowed, we also need to advocate the flow of information upward to places of influence, power, wealth, and intellectual elitism. These forces and resources at the top will not easily be shared.

It should be noted that this new paradigm or framework for the 21st century has supporters in all segments of society. In E. F. Shumacher's classic book, *Small is Beautiful* (1973), he states that the task of mobilizing relevant knowledge to help people help themselves is a task that requires money, but not very much. Rather, it is the thinking and method of operating that has to be changed. Two thirds of the world's population (more than three billion people) live in small villages. The World Health Organization rightly promotes the "district" or local level as the operational unit for delivery of primary health care, for the economic well-being of a locality is closely intertwined with its quality of life and community health.

Intersectoral cooperation (meaning all sectors, such as local businesses, religious organizations, civic groups, schools, political leaders, active citizens, and development organizations), fostered by common-goal agreement, is the most effective way to improve well-being from the bottom up. Localities define what their needs and values are, not the central and intermediate levels of government, which instead should act as facilitators so localities can meet their goals.

This new paradigm thus organizes better information sharing among smaller units—ultimately, individuals in communities—that are active in developing community well-being. And McDonald is on target in perceiving this new paradigm in the social worker's role as economic information entrepreneur. For this role to work well, partnering professions cannot always act as separate entities, but must interact along with all caring professions and the people to whom we have a responsibility. Social responsibility starts at the local level and moves outward. Only then can we act in an effective and culturally sensitive way.

References

Scitovsky, T. (1990). The benefits of asymmetric markets. *Journal of Economic Perspectives, 4*, 135-148.

Shumacher, E. F. (1973). *Small is beautiful.* London: Blond and Briggs.

11

Akwesasne Women: Meeting the Challenge of Environmental Threats

Adapted from a proposal by Katsi Cook

Akwesasne, a Native American community of 10,000 Mohawk people in northern New York state, lies downstream from some of the nation's most serious pollution. At Akwesasne, unemployment is a distressing 71%, and traditional subsistence on an agricultural economy is made poorer by environmental degradation. The crisis facing the Akwesasne people is shared by many indigenous people— community underdevelopment compounded by industrial overde-velopment. The degradation of the environment is seen by many as an assault on basic rights to health, identity, and cultural survival. As studies of the environment in and around the Akwesasne community have made evident, contamination poses a serious health threat because the Akwesasne people represent the top of the food chain. Locally caught fish and wildlife have been, and continue to be, major sources of protein in the traditional diet of this community in the Great Lakes Basin, and many of the fish swim in contaminated waters. Mothers under the care of nurse and mid-wife Katsi Cook were concerned about breastfeeding and about the potential for miscarriages and birth defects. Their concern led to the creation of a special program that focused on the pediatric, psychological, and clinical implications of environmental contamination of human milk.

The Akwesasne Mother's Milk Project was created with the involvement of these community members. Significantly, the project was implemented at the community level with the guiding principle that Mohawk mothers were active participants and co-investigators in the study. Field staff hired from the community became participants in the study, and were trained in breastfeeding peer counseling so that they could assist and support the mothers with whom they worked.

A fundamental principle of Mohawk healing relationships and behavior is reciprocity. However, opportunities for reciprocal interaction are limited by the asymmetrical paradigm of Western science, in which the 'expert' lacks either the willingness or the ability to convey belief in the ability of patients to contribute knowledge, as well. Adapting the Western model in Native communities contributes to the oppression experienced by Native people; because they have been treated for generations as objects and not life subjects, they can have difficulty attaining self-care and self-management.

One strength of this community-directed research design and its nine years of breast milk studies is the promotion of the belief that the Native people are capable of modifying their lives in positive ways. Mohawk mothers involved in the study learned of potential effects of contamination to their children, and they altered their behaviors accordingly. They decreased the amount of fish that they ate and reported healthier lifestyles, including declines in smoking, alcohol consumption, use of prescription drugs (other than vitamins and iron), and caffeinated coffee.

The Akwesasne Mother's Milk Project evolved into a multidisciplinary study at a toxic waste site. Researchers were invited to hold their meetings in the Akwesasne community, because all professionals who deliver services to communities should strive to learn from the experience of the people they serve, especially when those services are delivered across cultures. Cultural competency training for professionals must be encouraged by the consumers of research findings.

This project also gave rise to the First Environment Project, a Native American women's environmental health, education, networking, and outreach venture. From the concerns of Mohawk women grew a major Superfund Basic Research Program and the development of a model of community participation that empowered the community to respond to the myriad economic, social, and cultural problems of environmental degradation. The First Environment Project focuses on the development of Native women's environmental leadership and outreach to other Native communities in the Great Lakes region. Its newsletter serves as a networking tool and as a vehicle that encourages dialogue among Native American women and their communities, and it documents relationships between traditional Native American culture, community, and the environment. Re-identification of Native American people with their culture is a fundamental value of this project, and it is considered a step toward good health. Collaboration with community health programs like the St. Regis Mohawk Health

Services has enabled the women of Akwesasne to learn from the observations of mothers participating in the breast milk study, as befitting their own health needs. This has led them to develop culturally appropriate health components, such as the Empowering Young Mothers program to secure an intergenerational family health model.

It is hoped that these efforts can be expanded into more health education projects that will focus on enhancing community health. Future projects might include a weekly radio show; educational materials (such as brochures and posters), and a newsletter that would focus on environmental hazards inside and outside the home and inform community members of ongoing health research findings at Akwesasne. An ongoing community health assessment process would also be helpful. Although radio and print media might be good at reaching people in initial stages of awareness, interpersonal channels become critical in reinforcing attitudes and behaviors to bring about health-promoting activities. Environmental health fairs also can serve as an effective tool to educate the community about the environment.

Akwesasne has made, and will continue to make, a conscious effort to pool its thinking to create culturally cogent definitions, strategies, and solutions to the problem of toxic contamination of the environment. The community will continue its investigation into the impact of exposure to hazardous waste until an environmental health portrait of a community at risk is complete across generations and across gender. Unfortunately, contamination will remain, even from cleaned-up sites, as long as the St. Lawrence River flows.

12

Collaboration and Community-Based Strategies for Individuals and Families in Rural Areas

Katharine Briar-Lawson and Hal A. Lawson

Drawing upon findings and lessons learned from site visits in 35 states, we will emphasize in this chapter the need to integrate service strategies with economic and community development strategies. We will then explore possibilities for building more integrative approaches to economic, employment, and occupational supports.

A growing number of today's collaborative initiatives build multisector university–community partnerships. Up to 80 universities[1] have begun leadership preparation programs for collaborative practices and organizational partnerships (e.g., Brandon, 1996; Casto & Julia, 1994; Gardner, 1996; Lawson, 1996, 1997; Lawson & Hooper-Briar, 1994; see also Jivanjee, Moore, Schultze, & Friesen, 1995). Many of the universities involved in interprofessional education and training initiatives have committed to community partnerships and other field-based, education, and research strategies (Brandon & Meuter, 1995). Many universities are also presently involved in categorical partnerships involving, for example, schools of social work partnered with child welfare agencies, schools of education with public schools, or schools of public health with community health organizations.

We now are ready for what we call a second generation of interprofessional and cross-systems partnerships (Hooper-Briar & Lawson, 1996). In this era, university-related disciplines like archi-

---

[1] Although the term "university" is used throughout, we are not excluding four-year and community colleges that have professional education programs and partnerships with local communities.

tecture, nursing, public administration, social work, education, law, and recreation–leisure might be working toward a common core of content. This core may include: empowerment, cultural competence, congruence, family-centered practice, economic development, income supports, occupational development, and job creation. Collaborating disciplines might have the equivalent of a governor's cabinet in the provost's office which funds cross-disciplinary core courses, research, and demonstration projects. An interprofessional code of ethics will also need to be developed. Community leaders and their local collaboratives would then be joined by university faculty and students, who can help with needs assessments, service delivery, and evaluation. Students' knowledge and skills are also enriched as they engage in service-based learning and data-based term papers.

Universities that serve cities are being called upon to be more responsive to the economic, employment, and occupational needs of their respective regions. Ira Harkavy at the University of Pennsylvania and the West End Philadelphia Improvement Corps has been a leader in the creation of a new university–community partnerships program at the U.S. Department of Housing and Urban Development (e.g., Benson & Harkavy, 1994, 1997; Harkavy & Puckett, 1994). In this program, 10 university–community partnerships receive grants each year; approximately 20 have been funded to date.

Despite these developments, the need remains to (a) expand this work to include rural communities and the universities serving them; (b) connect and integrate service-oriented, interprofessional strategies with economic development strategies; and (c) adopt results-oriented accountability frameworks as a way to ensure that the needs of individuals, families, and communities remain the top priority (Gardner, 1996).

Integrating Economic Development and Service Strategies

As a new century dawns, the calls for systems reforms involving helping professions can be heard from all sectors of society. The findings from funders investing in some of these reforms, such as the Annie E. Casey Foundation (1995) and the Ford Foundation (see Larner, Halpern, & Harkavy, 1992), provide an important reminder: *If root cause issues like economic, employment, and income supports for individuals, families, and communities go unaddressed, many change agendas will fail, or not achieve all of their goals.*

Such a message is not new to social work. Unfortunately, like many professions, social work has drifted away from preparing students for public-sector community practice, especially community economic development, employment, and occupational development (Specht & Courtney, 1994; Weil, 1996).

Poverty, Unemployment, Underemployment, and Economic Stress

Rural poverty may be aggravated by the demise of resource-based economies. These economic conditions persist in areas where a company or resource-based industry such as mining, timber, farming, or fishing dominates a town or community. When such industries close, the entire community can be devastated.

Families may be unable to afford their homes, and both property values and property taxes decline. Homes are repossessed as mortgage foreclosures increase. And as tax revenues decline, governments cut back spending on police, health, and social services (Briar, 1988). These and other economic costs are tied to profound human costs (Briar, 1988; Hooper-Briar & Lawson, 1995), including increased occurrences of homelessness (O'Flaherty, 1996).

Rural poverty often leads to "ripple effects" such as depression, self-recrimination, drug and alcohol use, child and spouse abuse, and stress-related health disorders. Economic stress caused by long-term economic insecurity, job loss, and underemployment may lead to attachment to vigilante and right-wing groups and increases in school failures and dropouts, teen pregnancy, juvenile delinquency, abductions, satanic cult worship, and violent behavior. In some cases, poverty, unemployment, and economic stress become intergenerational family challenges, resulting in blocked aspirations, apathy, and despair (Briar, 1988; Larner, Halpern, & Harkavy, 1992). Despite the complexity and severity of these challenges, individuals and families in rural areas also demonstrate resiliency, strengths, and high aspirations.

Beyond Welfare

Until recently, many individuals and families in rural communities have relied upon the welfare system. Welfare reform now brings new barriers to personal, family, and community recovery. In particular, many mothers are among the most vulnerable parents encountering the current welfare-to-work requirements. In the past, they have stabilized their care-giving and provider roles by raising their children on welfare. Without meaningful employment opportunities, removal of welfare assistance may require these women and others to accept short-term, sporadic "twilight" jobs that leave them and their children worse off because of the combined effects of underemployment, the absence of medical and other personnel benefits, and the costs of child care. These same women may have been victimized by abusive relationships, and other adults in their lives may have suffered on their own from the human costs of layoffs and prolonged joblessness. Such stressors take their toll on women caregivers, which they may cope with through alcohol use, depression, or abuse of loved ones (Briar, 1988).

Losing a job and then experiencing multiple rejections during subsequent job searches can render employable persons unemployable, because they become discouraged and immobilized. Mothers, again, are vulnerable as they compete for jobs, experience rejection, and encounter the terror of losing their welfare benefits and their children. It is predicted that out-of-home placements for children will rise, as will the cost of the child welfare system. In fact, many states are expecting an increase in foster care as a result of welfare reform. Collaboratives can and should mitigate the stress that the most vulnerable women and children will endure. Absent these strategies, some may find this process so disabling that they become eligible for Supplementary Security Insurance. Others, especially women and children, may be forced to cope through drug dealing or related survival strategies.

Collaborative Practices Defined and Justified

Collaboration is not an end in itself; it is merely one means (albeit an important one) to improve individual and family well-being. Collaboration occurs when no one profession or organization can achieve its goals without building upon its interdependence with others. Here are the essential elements of collaboration that we and others propose (e.g., Bruner, 1996; Gardner, 1996):

- shared agreement about problem domain(s);
- shared aims, values, change principles, and improvement strategies;
- shared results and accountability;
- shared commitment to monitoring results and making adjustments when barriers are identified;
- shared information and resources;

- opportunities for calculated risk-taking, role release, and continued learning;
- democratized leadership and decision-making structures, including structures that involve community members as well as helping professionals;
- shared commitments, expressed in interagency agreements, to needed changes in policies, organizational structures and cultures, and definitions of "optimal practices."

In this perspective, collaboration is tailored to local contexts and becomes embedded in them. To aid in this process, service providers may relocate under one roof at a school, such as in school-based service configurations, or in a neighborhood, such as a family resource center. To promote systems integration, middle managers across systems and agencies meet to reorganize frontline staff to streamline the process of accessing flexible funds, dealing with eligibility problems, and so forth. Collaboratives also involve executives of educational, health, and social service systems who may meet monthly or quarterly to examine common optimal practices, policies, and funding strategies to promote family-centered, community-oriented practices. Conflicting values are addressed and realignment of agency policy is touted as consistent with new and more comprehensive service approaches. Interagency and intersystem agreements are written to forge and reinforce these partnerships, and outcomes for success are defined in cross-systems terms. For example, child welfare agencies might assume more responsibility and concern for a child's educational success and a parent's job acquisition. Or, a school might assume more responsibility for child welfare, family support, and preservation (Lawson, 1995; Lawson & Briar-Lawson, 1997). In brief, mutual accountability for shared outcomes is one measure of success for advanced collaborations.

Rationale for Collaboration and Consumer-Guided Approaches

We know that responding to challenged families can involve a dozen or more service providers who often do not communicate and inadvertently undercut one another's case plan.[2] Many families are stymied by top–down professional mandates and case plans;

---

[2] Gardner (1996) reports over 50 agencies were involved in his family's adoption cases.

they feel left out in decision making and disenfranchised in the helping process. Many may find that their problems, needs, and, above all, their aspirations and strengths are neither heard nor addressed.

Some collaborative practices are consumer guided or family driven. There are numerous advantages to this approach (Alameda, 1996; Hooper-Briar & Lawson, 1994, 1996), in which individuals and families are viewed as experts in their own lives, meriting shared power over decisions that affect them. Their presenting problems and individual needs are also viewed in terms of family and community capacity building.

Consumer-guided collaborative practices do not eliminate the need for specialized, professional expertise. Nor does the collaborative movement mean that specialists will be replaced by generalists. The search for more effective, integrative strategies that improve well-being and reduce human suffering does, however, require four related changes:

1. Accepting the expert knowledge of vulnerable individuals and families and using their knowledge to fill gaps in current case plans;

2. Responding to social support and resource needs—such as jobs, transportation, or child care—without abandoning conventional service technologies;

3. Searching for community-based strategies to alleviate economic insecurity and stress, unemployment, underemployment, and poverty;

4. Recognizing that there will never be enough professionals, and hence finding ways to employ community residents as paraprofessionals who help solve individual and family problems while building community capacities (Alameda, 1996; Hooper-Briar & Lawson, 1994, 1996; Larner, Halpern, & Harkavy, 1992).

These changes recast the roles of professionals; by providing a shared foundation for practice, they change the parameters of specialization.

Rural Economic and Community Development

Findings from rural capacity-building efforts demonstrate that the same factors that account for effectiveness in collaboratives for children, youth, and families are also requisites for effective community economic development. These factors include: vision-driven work, acceptance and commitment to change, vertical and horizontal linkages with other collaboratives, and dispersed leadership roles (McGuire, Rubin, Agranoff, & Richards, 1994). In fact, one predictor of success in rural areas is the extent to which the community can adjust and adapt to controversy and conflict. Thus, conflict management strategies, which are also important in social and health service collaboratives, can be transferred and adapted to the community economic development strategy. Skills in needs assessment, market analysis, and self-promotion are now common in the burgeoning private practice movements of our once poverty-oriented social work profession. Private practitioners, too, can be useful resources because of their applicable business skills.

Community asset- and strength-mapping, in turn, has become an extension of current social work approaches to ecomapping. Kretzmann and McKnight (1993) focus our attention on assets rather than deficits, on mapping community strengths to build capacities rather than to impose top–down solutions that may or may not be sought or desired. Their work builds on a strengths-based resilience analysis that is also moving to center stage in helping fields like social work and education.

Within the framework of local community practice, we suggest a series of possible interventions and approaches that could be mounted by our collaborating professions. As Figure 1 reflects, we start with local development and self-help initiatives, move to social action, and end with top–down planning and trickle-down models. These three domains are consistent, as well, with the conceptual models in community organization and community development discussed by Jones (1996).

Local and Self-Help Strategies

At the local level, there is a sketchy patchwork of employment services; the most promising are "job clubs." Based on the Weight Watchers model of intensive group support, workers spend two weeks going through the yellow pages, cold-calling employers and sending in applications. It is estimated that welfare recipients may need to submit 99 applications to get 15 interviews to land one job. Job club groups also barter haircuts, clothing, and transportation for their participants. Despite their relative success, job clubs are not offered as basic entitlements or services. Job search workshops, of less intensity and involving perhaps a three-hour seminar, may more routinely reflect the state of job-seeking supports. Both job

Figure 1. A Summary of Key Strategies for Rural Areas

Integrating Community Economic Development, Occupational Development, and Employment

Locality Development and Self-Help

- Enterprise and empowerment zones.
- Job search and job placement strategies: self-help, job clubs.
- Microenterprise development; local employment initiatives in which agencies and other institutions become incubators for jobs (as groups in Australia advocate); loan and finance models such as those created by Grameen Bank (Pakistan).
- Building communities from the inside out (Kretzmann & McKnight, 1993), starting with assets and strengths and aiming for strong social support networks and greater economic self-sufficiency; examples include local credit and loan associations, mutual assistance networks, and barter/exchange systems (such as at the Grace Hill settlement house in St. Louis, MO).

Social Action Initiatives

- Job protection strategies.
- Taxes and compensation for production industry closures in community.
- Union agreements and strikes for jobs,
- Closure prevention plans (e.g., leveraged buyouts by employees); collaborative ownership strategies (e.g., buyouts of companies and corporations using employee benefits and payroll contributions); social action and industrial social work strategies to advance job retention and job sharing and to minimize disruptions to workforce, families, and community.
- Action to redirect loan funds to low-income individuals and communities.

Social Planning and Technical Assistance

- Job Training and Partnership Act—training and job placement models for targeted groups.
- Venture-capital collaboratives; securing loans for investments.
- Approved use of unemployment benefits.
- Job creation through economic stimuli.
- Job creation through employer subsidies and tax credits; new welfare reform strategy.
- Government creates public sector jobs through programs like the Comprehensive Employment Training Act.
- Other training programs.

clubs and job search workshops assume that jobs are available and that those with skills are more likely to get them.

In rural communities, some collaboratives have started out in schools since schools are often the hubs of communities.[3] Parents ride the school buses with their children and are able then to get GEDs, apply for social services, get job counseling, and learn new skills, perhaps as microenterprise entrepreneurs at their local school. Some parents are also employed as paraprofessional teachers and service providers (Briar-Lawson, Lawson, Collier, & Joseph, 1997; Briar-Lawson, Rooney, Lawson, Alameda, White, Radina, & Herzog, 1997). Others are employed as receptionists, custodians, and cafeteria workers. Ideally, occupational ladders are developed for these parents. They start off in jobs like these, and after seeking training in community colleges and universities, they accept other jobs. When these initial parents leave, others are recruited and trained in their place. Meaningful employment for these parents often has beneficial effects on their children, including school performance and healthy development (e.g., Haveman & Wolfe, 1995). Rural high schools involved in community and economic development also report the invaluable resource that these efforts represent (Versteg, 1993).

School-based collaboratives are not restricted to rural areas either. At Intermediate School 218 in New York City (Washington Heights), the Children's Aid Society invested $1 million in a school–community development strategy. The children clear over $40,000 a year from their school store.

Another approach that has great promise—but has not often been implemented with state and federal funds—is local enterprise and family business development. In Australia, Canada, and parts of Western Europe, intensive supports to foster job creation though loans, collectives, and cooperatives have shown great merit (Briar, 1988). In Australia, such investments have been called Local Employment Initiatives, or LEIs. Social service agencies cooperate with groups of displaced workers whose livelihoods have been permanently lost to new markets in developing nations. Agencies bring in these groups to do local needs assessments, after which they learn to design their own local businesses to meet local and

---

[3] We have recently started integrating school and community strategies that connect school reform, health care reform, child welfare reform, and community development. One way is a planned project for Family-Supportive Community Schools (Lawson & Briar-Lawson, 1997).

regional needs. Grant funds and loans are all secured through the agency, which serves as a mediator and advocate.

Lessons also are being harvested from Grameen Bank's approaches to loans for poor women in developing nations, in this case Pakistan. In the past, a form of red-lining has denied loans to low-income persons. Such practices can be countered with the evidence of high repayment rates and the revolving loan concept. Because of the reliable repayment rate on small, revolving loan funds, banks like Chicago's South Shore Bank are offering such services and loans to low-income individuals and families. On the other hand, sometimes Community Development Block Grant funds have been used for gentrification, and poor individuals and families have been displaced. Much more work needs to be done to secure such loans for the poor, especially where rural communities are concerned, since these were funds designed for them when community development strategies emerged in the 1960s.

Finally, there are nonmonetarized ways to provide services, supports, and resources for vulnerable individuals and families. For example, we draw upon the model used in an exemplary community development strategy from Grace Hill, a settlement house in St. Louis. Here neighbors have an extensive computerized bartering system with credit cards that record the "time dollar" hours they have contributed to one another's well-being. These "time dollars" fuel a mutual-aid economy not dependent upon money.

Merging Consumer-Guided Collaborative Practices with Employment Ladders

For the past six years, we have been testing and attempting to replicate a bottom–up employment strategy that also serves as a child welfare, school reform, welfare reform, and economic reform strategy. This has involved a low-income group of women in South Miami Beach, Florida, called the RAINmakers (for their *referral and information network*). Beginning in 1990 they were trained to be paraprofessional educators, social service workers, and health and housing aides; today these women run their own agency and have recently opened a day care center. Once deemed very challenged women and families, they are now heralded for their contributions to the Miami Beach community. Instead of facing profound income and language barriers, they have organized mutual assistance, eviction improvements, and microenterprise supports for children, youth, and families. In addition, they have helped to transform a school that was once so impoverished that six years ago the Dade County School System targeted it to receive a Danforth

Foundation grant. Today, rather than being among the most challenged, this school has received an award from the state as one of its two top Title One schools.[4] Achievement scores have doubled each year, and family stabilization has also increased (Alameda, 1996).

We also recruited women and men in recovery from crack cocaine to be frontline service providers for those who had already given birth to a substance-exposed newborn. These frontline practitioners, like the RAINmakers, brought about such high success rates that not only have they been acclaimed for their work, but their employment has become full time. Like their counterparts, several have already gone on to college. Once overtaken by the effects of poverty, depression, and isolation, they have been able to "ladder off" of welfare rather than being thrown from it and devastated irreparably by lack of income or job supports. Given the ongoing welfare crisis, these models offer promise for assisting the most vulnerable recipients.

We can build on models such as RAINmakers and others and tie paraprofessional roles to school and child welfare reforms, as parents reach out to one another and help with children's schooling and development and provide support to prevent them from being placed in foster care. The parents we seek to help may be the ones that, without such support and investment, later become hardship cases or lose their children to foster care. Pilot programs need to be initiated that recruit, train, and fund low-income parents for paraprofessional work as teacher aides, social service employees, or parent and child welfare aides. Local communities and universities can generate a "welfare reform" plan that includes appropriate education, training, and long-term occupational ladders.

Social Action Strategies

Some of the work to be done cannot be advanced without advocacy and transformational change strategies. Collaboratives have found that community change often requires group-based collective action—whether it involves fighting for a traffic light to

---

[4] Title One is a U.S. Department of Education classification for schools in which the majority of children qualify for free and reduced lunch programs. These schools receive special subsidies to improve learning. Under the new regulations, Title One Schools are required to use some of their funding to employ parents, and parents must participate in decision making about other funding and program decisions. These new provisions for parent empowerment are not well-publicized and appear not to be widely implemented.

protect children or redirecting loan money to aid the poor. These collective actions are the product of stakeholders coming together and committing to better outcomes for individuals, families, and communities. The movement to build collaboratives around the country is one facet of social change and community development that offers promise for these times. Driven by vision statements and consumers of the change process, heads of agencies, in concert with college and university representatives, commit to a set of improved outcomes. Barrier-busting then becomes the process by which outcomes are incrementally achieved.[5]

Other social action has stemmed from increasing awareness of the relationship between globalization, de-industrialization, technological change, economic stress, and human costs (Danzinger & Gottschalk, 1995). For example, concerted efforts have been made to stop plant closures and farm closures; labor unions have tried to prevent out-contracting by corporations; and companies and corporations have been retained through citizen or employee buyout strategies or through collectives or cooperatives becoming local owners and community-accountable stakeholders. Holding companies accountable for employment and economic practices has resulted in charging corporations for costs to displaced families when they relocate.

Social Planning: Beyond Trickle-Down Approaches

At the federal and state levels, enterprise and empowerment zones represent some of the planned investments in poor communities (Riposa, 1996). While some rural communities now benefit from these funds, much greater investments are needed. Empowerment zone funds help to integrate social services and school and economic development, and they offer the greatest promise for the integrative practices of the future. The selection of these communities for reinvestment dollars has been very political and obviously falls far short of need. President Clinton has also proposed community development loan strategies and has urged banks to aid in the rebuilding and job creation process. The fact remains, however, that these strategies have inherent limitations; they are related to top–down, trickle-down approaches in the private sector. Many

---

[5] Ideally, the more that data can be collected on barrier-busting, the greater the success. Evaluation, action planning, and decision-making are integrated participatory-action approaches that blend nicely with consumer-guided or family-driven collaborative practices.

communities trying to lure businesses have waived taxes in the hope that trickle-down job creation will occur. Person-centered job creation, rather than company-centered trickle-down economics, may be the preferred policy focus of the future.[6]

In Europe, welfare and unemployment benefits have gone directly to the employers which prospective workers find willing to hire them. Such personal leveraging of assets may be another tool to aid welfare recipients and jobless workers.

Conclusion

We are at a crossroads as a nation. The needs of rural communities are as important as those of urban communities. Unfortunately, too many rural communities and their children and families are neglected. Rebuilding rural communities requires new resources for this purpose. It necessitates integrated economic and employment strategies in combination with social supports and conventional services. Helping professionals who work in rural communities will need preparation for this work, and universities need to respond to this need. Preparation programs must emphasize knowledge, sensitivities, and skills for collaboration and integrated, community-based strategies tailored to the unique features of rural communities.

In brief, interprofessional education and training for rural communities will have some unique design features and content. Planning for rural communities helps advance the development of interprofessional education and training beyond "one size fits all" program models. Simultaneously, we must join forces to model collaboration in our universities as we form partnerships with local community collaboratives. Spearheading economically relevant, family-centered change will be our ongoing mission as we invent more proactive helping strategies for the nation.

References

Alameda, T. (1996). The healthy learners project: Bringing the community into the school. In K. Hooper-Briar & H. Lawson (Eds.), *Expanding partner-*

---

[6] Riposa (1996) provides a brief critique of trickle-down planning in enterprise zones and supports the value of social and educational infrastructures associated with new empowerment zones. Unfortunately, rural communities are again neglected in the discussion.

ships for vulnerable children, youth, and families (pp. 46-56). Alexandria, VA: Council on Social Work Education.

Annie E. Casey Foundation. (1995). *The path of most resistance.* Baltimore, MD: Author.

Benson, L., & Harkavy, I. (1994). 1994 as turning point: The university-assisted community school idea becomes a movement. *Universities and Community Schools, 4*(1-2), 5-8.

Benson, L., & Harkavy, I. (1997). School and community in the global society: A Neo-Deweyian theory of community problem-solving schools, cosmopolitan neighborly communities and a Neo-Deweyian "manifesto" to dynamically connect school and community. *Universities and Community Schools, 51*(1-2), 16-70.

Brandon, R. (1996). The collaborative services movement: Implications for national policymakers. In K. Hooper-Briar & H. Lawson (Eds.), *Expanding partnerships for vulnerable children, youth, and families* (pp. 322-346). Alexandria, VA: Council on Social Work Education.

Brandon, R., & Meuter, L. (Eds.). (1995). *Proceedings, national conference on interprofessional education and training.* Seattle, WA: Human Services Policy Center, University of Washington.

Briar, K. (1988). *Social work and the unemployed.* Silver Spring, MD: NASW Press.

Briar-Lawson, K., Lawson, H., Collier, C., & Joseph, A. (1997). School-linked comprehensive services: Promising beginnings, selected lessons learned and future challenges. *Social Work in Education, 19*(3).

Briar-Lawson, K., Rooney, B., Lawson, H., Alameda, T., White, L., Radina, M. E., & Herzog, K. (1997). *Creating family supportive community schools: A manual for improving parent involvement and empowerment.* Oxford, OH: Institute for Educational Renewal, Miami University.

Bruner, C. (1996). *Realizing a vision for children, families and neighborhoods: An alternative to other modest proposals.* Des Moines, IA: National Center for Service Integration, Child and Family Policy Center.

Casto, M., & Julia, M. (1994). *Interprofessional care and collaborative practice.* Pacific Grove, CA: Brooks/Cole.

Danzinger, S., & Gottschalk, P. (1995). *America unequal.* Cambridge, MA: Harvard University Press.

Gardner, S. (1996). *Beyond collaboration to results: Hard choices in the future of services to children and families.* Fullerton, CA: Center for Collaboration for Children, California State University.

Harkavy, I., & Puckett, J. (1994). Lessons from Hull House for the contemporary university. *Social Service Review, 68,* 299-319.

Haveman, R., & Wolfe, B. (1995). *Succeeding generations: On the effects of investments in children.* New York: Russell Sage Foundation.

Hooper-Briar, K., & Lawson, H. (1994). *Serving children, youth and families through interprofessional collaboration and service integration: A framework for action.* Oxford, OH: Institute for Educational Renewal, Miami University, and Danforth Foundation.

Hooper-Briar, K., & Lawson, H. (1995). Families and social development. *International Journal of Comparative and Social Welfare, 11*(1), 1-26.

Hooper-Briar, K., & Lawson, H. (Eds.). (1996). *Expanding partnerships for vulnerable children, youth, and families.* Alexandria, VA: Council on Social Work Education.

Jivanjee, P., Moore, K., Schultze, K., & Friesen, B. (1995). *Interprofessional education for family-centered services: A survey of interprofessional/interdisciplinary training programs.* Portland, OR: Portland State University, Research and Training Center on Family Support and Children's Mental Health.

Jones, S. (1996). *Collaboration and coordination regarding rural social work and economic development.* Unpublished manuscript, State University of New York at Albany.

Kretzmann, J., & McKnight, J. (1993). *Building communities from the inside out: A path toward finding and mobilizing a community's assets.* Chicago: ACTA Publications.

Larner, M., Halpern, R., & Harkavy, O. (Eds.). (1992). *Fair start for children: Lessons learned from seven demonstration projects.* New Haven, CT: Yale University Press.

Lawson, H. (1995). Schools and educational communities in a new vision for child welfare. *Journal for a Just and Caring Education, 1*(1), 5-26.

Lawson, H. (1996). Developing interprofessional education programs: Definitions, assumptions, content, and principles. In K. Hooper-Briar & H. Lawson (Eds.), *Expanding partnerships for vulnerable children, youth, and families* (pp. 181-195). Alexandria, VA: Council on Social Work Education.

Lawson, H. (1997). Children in crisis, the helping professions and the social responsibilities of universities. *Quest, 49*(1), 8-33.

Lawson, H., & Briar-Lawson, K. (1997). Toward family-supportive community schools. In C. Day, D. van Veen, & G. Walraven (Eds.), *Children and youth at risk and urban education: Research, policy and practice* (pp. 181-208). Leuven/Apeldoorn: The European Educational Research Association and Garant Academic Publishers.

Lawson, H., & Hooper-Briar, K. (1994). *Expanding partnerships: Involving colleges and universities in interprofessional collaboration and service integration.* Oxford, OH: Institute for Educational Renewal, Miami University, and Danforth Foundation.

McGuire, M., Rubin, B., Agranoff, R., & Richards, C. (1994). Building development capacity in nonmetropolitan communities. *Public Administration Review, 54,* 406-423.

O'Flaherty, B. (1996). *Making room: The economics of homelessness.* Cambridge, MA: Harvard University Press.

Riposa, G. (1996). From enterprise zones to empowerment zones: The community context of urban economic development. *American Behavioral Scientist, 39,* 536-551.

Specht, H., & Courtney, M. (1994). *Unfaithful angels: How social work has abandoned its mission.* New York: Free Press.

Versteg, D. (1993). The rural high school as community resource. *Educational Leadership, 50,* 54-55.

Weil, M. (1996). Community building: Building community practice. *Social Work, 41,* 481-500.

13

Interagency Collaboration and Coordination: Implications for Professional Development

Kathleen A. O'Brien

Reverend Leon Sullivan, a national leader in the area of community-based employment of the disadvantaged, provides a parable to show why many youth remain unemployed despite the various organizations and agencies that attempt to resolve youth employment difficulties (Institute for Educational Leadership, 1986, p. 1):

> A boy trapped in a deep hole called for help. Several adults ran to his aid, each offering rope for him to haul himself out, but each rope was too short. There was the "rope" of the public school system—old and tough and hard to handle. There was the employment and training "rope," new but thin and fragile. There was a higher education "rope," too far away for him to reach, the labor union "rope," the "rope" of the business community and others. There was no shortage of ropes, but still the boy could not be saved.
> "*Tie your ropes together,*" the boy said, "and let them down to me!*"

As the parable suggests, effective redress of complex social problems requires the input of multiple social service agencies. Kirst and McLaughlin (1989) argue that "the current fragmentation of children's services represents a fundamental failure to confront the comprehensive needs of children, youth and adults" (p. 2). They further contend that single-service agencies rarely have the capacity or the resources necessary to deal with multiple and diverse client needs. For these reasons, the coordination of service delivery rather than independent agency action is increasingly recommended (Hallett & Stevenson, 1980; Melaville & Blank, 1991) and, in some cases, mandated (Kirst & McLaughlin, 1989).

Interagency coordination of services to support the homeless is critical, because it serves the multiple needs of homeless children, who, studies have shown, are more likely than other children to suffer malnutrition (National Coalition for the Homeless, 1987) and educational and psychological problems (Bassuk & Rubin, 1987). They are more likely than other children to attend school irregularly and to change schools (Child Welfare League of America, 1987; Jackson, 1988). The U.S. Department of Health and Human Services (1992) estimates that as many as one third of all homeless children do not attend school regularly. Some educational agencies have joined with human service agencies to ensure that education is provided to all children and that the varied needs of homeless children are met.

This chapter reviews the qualitative results of a study of interorganizational relationships among human service agencies that provide services to homeless children and youth in nine New York State communities.[1] Guidelines for effective coordination and collaborative practices are provided, and implications for professional development are explored.

Interorganizational Relationships

Qualitative analysis found that five out of the nine groups of community agencies appeared to have mixed perceptions of relational effectiveness, while the other four had mostly productive, mutual feelings of relational effectiveness among themselves. Two of the latter four communities had New York State Education Department grants awarded to their local Board of Cooperative Educational Services to coordinate interagency planning efforts among schools, shelters, the Department of Social Services, and other agencies on behalf of the area homeless population. The other two communities had either a coordinating and case management agency or a Homeless Coordinator in a school district who linked services among area agencies serving homeless children and youth. The four communities with more effective interagency coordination also had agencies working together to develop and implement student service plans, and these agencies indicated they wanted to better evaluate the outcomes of these plans.

---

[1] These relationships were originally studied using qualitative and quantitative analyses (see also O'Brien, 1996).

The remaining communities responded that the number of services in the area and/or the comprehensiveness of service delivery were other advantages to interagency coordination. Agency contacts also noted that service gaps often centered on transitional services for homeless teens and young adults and on transportation difficulties from shelters to schools.

Coordination among agencies often resulted in shared information, pooled resources, and/or joint funding of services or personnel, results show. Concerns about the confidentiality of homeless clients, however, sometimes limited the information shared, and community agency liaisons expressed strong concerns about the threat of reduced or eliminated funding. High staff turnover was also cited as a barrier to coordination.

Agency contacts seemed to gravitate toward liaison staff that demonstrated follow-through and commitment to homeless clients and toward those trusted by other agency contacts. Across the board, agency contacts said that having professionals in key liaison positions made coordination work. The agency contacts focused less on specific professional expertise and more on professionals' positive interpersonal traits, such as an ability to work with others and to develop trusting relationships.

Other research has studied what happens when various professionals attempt to work with each other. Hall (1986) contends that service delivery professionals experience decreased effectiveness in situations where many types of professionals are found. Melaville and Blank (1991) add that the current system—a mix of private and public agencies—inadequately meets the needs of children and families due to a lack of functional communication among agency contacts coping with significant differences in institutional mandates and professional orientation. Agencies involved in service coordination and collaboration must recognize their similarities and differences in professional orientation and develop effective communication strategies among themselves to more effectively meet the needs of those they serve.

The Center for the Study of Social Policy (CSSP) (1995) documents "New Futures," an ambitious five-year, $50 million, multiple site evaluation of five low-income communities sponsored by the Annie E. Casey Foundation. New Futures aimed to measurably improve school achievement, increase employment after high school, and lessen adolescent pregnancy and school dropout rates. The project's core strategy involved developing in each community a newly formed interagency governing group, called a collaborative, that would revive and restructure organizations serving youth and rebuild fragmented service systems. After five years, New Futures cities did not measurably decrease dropout, teen pregnancy, or unemployment rates, but they did improve student academic performance. Collaboratives were unsuccessful in developing comprehensive action plans that went beyond the discrete activities of individual community organizations. The CSSP's researchers recommend that future community-based collaboratives institute "ongoing strategic operational planning" (p. XIII). Five years does not seem enough time to demonstrate clear, measurable outcomes, however, since communities have little practical knowledge about how to change agency and interorganizational operations.

I strongly recommend that proven practices of coordination and collaboration among organizations be studied and documented, and that this information be widely disseminated to higher education institutions and human service agencies. This information is critical to train new members of the helping professions and retrain professionals already working in social agencies and schools. Community agencies are thirsting for leadership and support in learning quality approaches to working with one another.

Guidelines for Best Practices

Melaville and Blank (1991) list several determinants of successful collaborative efforts, such as: the community climate where initiatives start; the policies and procedures that support or inhibit trust building and conflict resolution; the individuals involved in collaborating; and the resources available to support initiatives. Guthrie (1996) provides a well-written, clearly understandable book, *How to Coordinate Services for Students and Families,* that articulates a nine-step program guide to developing interagency coordination. The steps include identifying programs currently offered in the community or local area and surveying the availability and current status of services within the programs. The basic needs of children and families are reviewed in terms of how services are accessed and whether service gaps or overlaps exist. Collaborators need to create a common vision, Guthrie says; they need to develop goals with expectations of achievements and design needed comprehensive services. Guthrie recommends developing a plan incorporating formative and summative evaluation procedures, with the last of the nine steps involving plan implementation.

Mitchell and Scott (1994, p. 77) add that the following components of integrated service delivery eliminate fragmentation and serve as a framework for evaluating interorganizational collaboration:

- professional norms developed to lift agency staff beyond skillful application of their expertise, focusing attention on the underlying character of client needs;

- interdisciplinary norms of professional cooperation able to guide consultation and decision making among professions with different types of expertise;

- institutional norms and procedures robust enough to guide each interagency case management and organizational resource allocation.

Bass (1992) identifies the essential aspects of coordinated, comprehensive service delivery to runaway and homeless youth. These components serve as a model for all forms of interagency coordination. She agrees with Guthrie that a community needs to determine the education, health, and social service agencies involved and develop cooperative agreements among agencies. Bass focuses on targeting individuals who need to be accessed via outreach activities and calls for the creation of public-awareness activities.

Bass also recommends that identified at-risk youth and their families should be given the power to develop, implement, and evaluate services for themselves. She joins Guthrie in suggesting procedures to assess the needs of targeted populations and in recommending the development, implementation, and evaluation of service plans at regular intervals. Bass additionally recommends ongoing strategic planning to create and maintain needed services and staff training.

A national network of individuals and universities is currently developing training in interprofessional education. The movement is based on the premise that human service professionals cannot be effective if they dwell only on aspects of the client that fit into their specific professional training (Cohen, 1996). The University of Washington Interprofessional Program focuses on the dynamics of working in groups, while the Interprofessional Commission of Ohio at Ohio State University provides interprofessional courses for graduate students and professionals in education, law, medicine, counseling, nursing, social work, psychology, and theology.

National network leaders (see Brandon & Meuter, 1995) state that interprofessional training should focus on a well-defined mission connected to enhanced outcomes for children, families, and communities. Schools such as Boston's Wheelock College and the Harvard project on Schooling and Children have recently created innovative, interdisciplinary courses and field work programs for undergraduates. Colleges and universities need to continue to develop collaborative approaches that educate professionals in various fields to work effectively with each other in providing comprehensive services to children and families.

At-risk children and families often come to our attention with diverse needs that demand a comprehensive service approach. Incoming and practicing professionals that work in the helping service fields need to effectively coordinate and collaborate with one another to best help children and families. A comprehensive service approach through coordinated and collaborative work offers the supportive network needy children and families require to improve their circumstances. No one should be in a deep hole of difficult circumstances and be offered only isolated services that fail to address that person's total basic needs.

References

Bass, D. (1992). *Helping homeless youths.* Washington, DC: NASW Press.

Bassuk, E. L., & Rubin, L. (1987). Homeless children: A neglected population. *American Journal of Orthopsychiatry, 141*(12), 1546-1550.

Brandon, R., & Meuter, L. (1995) *National conference on interprofessional education and training: Proceedings.* Seattle: Human Services Policy Center, University of Washington.

Center for the Study of Social Policy. (1995). *Building new futures for at-risk youth.* Washington, DC: Author.

Child Welfare League of America. (1987). *Study of the homeless children and families: Preliminary findings.* Washington, DC: Author.

Cohen, D. L. (1996, Feb. 28). A working relationship. *Education Week, 23,* 29-32.

Guthrie, L. F. (1996). *How to coordinate services for students and families.* Alexandria, VA: Association for Supervision and Curriculum Development.

Hall, R. H. (1986). Interorganizational or interprofessional relationships: A case of mistaken identity? In W. R. Scott & B. L. Black (Eds.), *The organization of mental health services, societal and community systems.* Beverly Hills, CA: Sage.

Hallett, C., & Stevenson, O. (1980). *Child abuse: Aspects of interprofessional cooperation.* London: Allen and Unwin.

Institute for Educational Leadership. (1986). *Metrolink—Developing human resources through metropolitan collaboration.* Washington, DC: Author.

Jackson, S. (1988). *The education rights of homeless children.* Cambridge, MA: Center for Law and Education.

Kirst, M. W., & McLaughlin, M. (1989, November). *Improving policies for children.* Paper presented for the Rockefeller Institute of Government, State University of New York, Albany.

Melaville, A. I., & Blank, M. J. (1991). *What it takes: Structuring interagency partnerships to connect children and families with comprehensive services.* Washington, DC: Education and Human Services Consortium.

Mitchell, D. E., & Scott, L. D. (1994). Professional and institutional perspectives on interagency collaboration. In L. Adler & S. Gardner (Eds.), *The politics of linking schools and social services.* Washington, DC: Palmer.

National Coalition for the Homeless (1987). *Broken lives: Denial of education of homeless children.* Washington, DC: Author.

O'Brien, K. A. (1996). *Interorganization cooperation and the effectiveness of service delivery to homeless children and youth.* Doctoral dissertation, State University of New York at Albany . (Available through University Microfilms International, Ann Arbor, MI 48106.)

U.S. Department of Health and Human Services, Office of Inspector General. (1992). *State and local perspectives on the McKinney Act.* Washington, DC: Author.

Conclusion

A Look Toward the Future: Lessons Learned

Joan Levy Zlotnik

The times in which we live are times of change. Public support for social programs is dwindling. The summer of 1996 brought about the first major change to the welfare system in 60 years with the creation of the Temporary Assistance to Needy Families (TANF) Program. It will take years to find out if this new social experiment will succeed, or if it will force more children into poverty, or if it will increase violence, homelessness, and substance abuse. Along with the welfare system, our health care system is changing, too. Managed care permeates the health care delivery system for those with private insurance and those receiving Medicare and Medicaid. Now managed care is beginning to affect the delivery of child welfare services, as well.

Technology remains a burgeoning force to be reckoned with. The accessibility of information from the internet shrinks the world for those who have access to it, and for people in rural communities, new technologies can provide stronger links to more populated communities. Interactive communication can provide a connection between those who were once isolated and those who are at the seat of information and resources.

As these changes take place, there is renewed attention to improving the delivery of health, education, and human services. Public interest has grown for increasing local community responsibility and for planning processes that work from the ground up, rather than the top down. Creating improved services is a particular challenge in rural communities with limited resources but a broad range of needs. As professional helpers, how do we best prepare for these changes and also help to lead, so that changes occur in the "right" directions to help enhance individual, family, and community well-being?

One of our greatest challenges is to predict the future: What will helping professionals look like in the 21st century? What kind of education and training will they need? What will be the role of the university in providing professional preparation, in providing ongoing training, in carrying out research and program development? How can communities and universities partner more effectively?

Out of shared interests in these questions, a commitment to collaboration and interprofessional work, and concern for professional education to meet these challenges, the Council on Social Work Education partnered with the School of Social Welfare, the School of Public Health, and the Institute for the Advancement of Health Care Management at the State University of New York at Albany to facilitate this innovative Focus Group meeting and to publish the papers from that meeting.

The focus group brought representatives of community organizations in health care and social services together with students, faculty, and academic administrators to examine the skills, values, and knowledge base necessary to prepare professional helpers—including doctors, nurses, educators, social workers, and public health specialists—to work in rural communities. Most of the participants had not worked together before, which reflects both the number of rural communities in New York and the diversity of the national leaders who came to share their perspectives. An incredible blending of ideas and information emerged, highlighting the value of and the ongoing need for collaboration among professional education programs within the university and among community and university groups. The important role of students as new professional leaders and key linkages to the community also emerged.

The meeting served as a model of interprofessional and community–university partnerships, bringing together diverse groups who developed a shared mission and shared agenda. Participants were energized by the combination of components brought together—the university with the community, the national perspective with local wisdom—as well as the individual interaction between social worker, educator, business major, association executive, physician, community organizer, local health provider, teacher, and public health specialist. Participants made an investment to sustain these connections and ideas beyond the meeting, and we hope that the preceding pages captured this for the reader and will help provide the reader with new tools and new ideas for better practices.

Collaboration, partnership, listening to and hearing from the community: these are all important themes which permeate these pages. As the teachings from the meeting and within these pages are analyzed, we hope the following points will be noted:

- the importance of involving the community in curriculum development;
- the value of a strengths-based perspective in direct practice and policy development;
- the applicability of a generalist approach to rural practice;
- the value of interprofessional education and practice;
- the role that students in field placements can play as the link between the community and the university;
- the importance of educating and involving legislators; and
- the need for university faculty to spend time in communities as researchers, practitioners, and program developers.

Another consistent theme that can be gathered from this effort is the importance of working from an interprofessional perspective. Whether community worker, community member, dean, college president, legislator, foundation project officer, government official, agency head, corporate executive, faculty member, or student, we should keep the following in mind as we prepare for the new millennium:

- Categorical funding of professional education may serve as a stumbling block to interprofessional education. We need to examine university incentives and funding strategies from the government, as well as foundations that support collaboration and address the elimination of barriers.
- Students need to be educated to work as a team with other professionals and with representatives of the community. They also need to acquire knowledge on common issues (i.e., child development), which can be acquired from an interdisciplinary class involving faculty from several programs teaching together.
- Students are often leaders in innovative practice and change.
- Interdisciplinary communication and collaboration are critical to successful professional development strategies.
- Involving the community, listening to the community, and allowing the community to lead in problem solving are critical components of successful collaboration.

- Respecting and valuing diversity is critical to successful collaboration.
- Leadership is important. University administrators, key faculty, legislators, community leaders, and agency directors need to support collaborative work.
- Change is a slow, evolutionary process. Commitment over the long term is necessary to achieve success.
- To create change, universities need to change their curricula, and practitioners in the community need to change their practice. Degree-based professional education and continuing education strategies must be developed. Field education opportunities and interactive, distance learning can provide important tools to prepare future practitioners and enhance the skills of current practitioners.

Recommendations for future actions revolve around what steps should occur in the university, in the community, and with community–university partnerships in order to successfully prepare professionals to work in the 21st century.

Recommendations for the University

- Work to develop a professional development curriculum for community practitioners.
- Reward interdisciplinary partnership efforts and remove partnership barriers in tenure decisions.
- Break down the categorical nature of discipline-specific studies.
- Share resources between professional schools for cooperative learning.
- Work community partnerships into the university mission.
- Utilize support from the deans of colleges and schools to continue collaborative learning projects.
- Form formal interprofessional relationships and agreements.

Recommendations for Communities

- Promote and become involved with associations created by the community.
- Extend resources to communities supporting local efforts, such as work groups seeking solutions for the community.
- Promote continual community professional development.
- Support community-based organizations.

Recommendations for Community–University Partnerships

- Professional associations should work with the university to create acceptance of faculty working in the community.
- The university should use the community as a teaching resource.
- The university should look at successful community partnership models (e.g., those developed by the W.K. Kellogg Foundation and the National Institute for Environmental Health Studies).
- University professionals and researchers should serve on community boards.
- The university should lend research and evaluation skills and resources to community collaboratives.
- The university and the community should be involved in each other's activities, creating mutuality.
- Universities should invite community leaders to conferences held by university and professional organizations, such as the NASW national conference.

National organizations, accrediting bodies, academic leaders, community-based organizations, legislatures, and community members all have a stake in ensuring that health and human services meet existing needs. Professional education and continuing education are critical tools in maintaining a well-prepared workforce, because learning is a continuous process and the world we live in is always changing. Internalizing the suggestions from this book and putting a strengths-based, community-focused, interprofessional agenda into action can help ensure individual, family, and community well-being and lead the university—in partnership with the community—into the 21st century.

Volume Contributors and Focus Group Invited Participants

Contributors

Katharine Briar-Lawson
Professor and Doctoral Program Head, School of Social Work
University of Utah, Salt Lake City, UT

Irene Cody
Graduate Student, School of Social Welfare
SUNY at Albany

Kristine Collins
Graduate Student, School of Social Welfare
SUNY at Albany

Katsi Cook
Clinical Instructor, School of Public Health
SUNY at Albany
Visiting Fellow, American Indian Program
Cornell University, Ithaca, NY

Joseph Davenport III
Private Practice
Columbia, MO

Judith A. Davenport
Professor, School of Social Work
University of Missouri, Columbia

Shirley J. Jones
Distinguished Service Professor, School of Social Welfare
SUNY at Albany

Hal A. Lawson
Professor, School of Social Work
University of Utah, Salt Lake City, UT

Patricia McDonald
Graduate Student, School of Social Welfare
SUNY at Albany

Gloria Meert
Program Director
W.K. Kellogg Foundation

Linda Mokarry
   Graduate Student, School of Social Welfare
   SUNY at Albany

Mark Morris
   Graduate Student, School of Social Welfare
   SUNY at Albany

Kathleen A. O'Brien
   Principal
   East Greenbush Central School, Albany, NY

Lorette Picciano
   Executive Director
   Rural Coalition, Washington, DC

Henry Pohl
   Associate Dean for Medical Education
   Albany Medical College

Gloria J. Reynolds
   Graduate Student, School of Public Health
   SUNY at Albany

Kim Rosekrans
   Graduate Student, School of Social Welfare
   SUNY at Albany

Ann Weick
   Dean, School of Social Welfare
   University of Kansas, Lawrence, KS

Dwight C. Williams
   Director, Leadership Institute, School of Public Health
   SUNY at Albany

Joan Levy Zlotnik
   Director of Special Projects
   Council of Social Work Education, Alexandria, VA

Discussants
Lillian Brannon
   Director, Center for Excellence in Learning and Teaching
   SUNY at Albany

Anne Fortune
   Associate Dean, School of Social Welfare
   SUNY at Albany

Richard Hall
  Distinguished Service Professor, Department of Sociology
  SUNY at Albany

James Izzo
  Graduate Student, School of Business
  SUNY at Albany

Marissa Panton
  Graduate Student, School of Business
  SUNY at Albany

Gloria J. Reynolds
  Graduate Student, School of Public Health
  SUNY at Albany

Joan Sinclair
  Commissioner
  Allegany County Department of Social Services, Belmont, NY

David Smingler
  Executive Assistant
  Office of Hugh Farley, New York State Senate, Albany, NY

Moderators
Shirley J. Jones

Mark Morris

Jo Ann Weatherwax
  Director, Institute for the Advancement of Health Care
  Management
  SUNY at Albany

Carol D. Young
  Director, Continuing Education, School of Public Health
  SUNY at Albany

Joan Levy Zlotnik

Focus Group Meeting

Professional Development of Helping Professions in Rural Communities: Trends for the 21st Century

Agenda

October 31, 1996

4:30–5:00p.m. ....Registration and
Reception for Presenters and Discussants

5:00–6:00p.m. .... Dinner

6:15–6:30p.m. ....

    Introductions .... Dr. Shirley Jones
    Greetings .... Dr. Carson Carr
Assistant Vice President for Student Services
and Director of EOP, University at Albany

6:30–7:45p.m. ....Student Presenters and
Discussants

Social Worker: An Economic Information Entrepreneur for the 21st Century

Presenter—Ms. Patricia McDonald
Graduate Student, School of Social Welfare
University at Albany
Discussant—Ms. Gloria Reynolds
Graduate Student, School of Public Health
University at Albany

Interagency Collaboration and Coordination: Implications for Professional Development

Presenter—Dr. Kathleen A. O'Brien
Recent Graduate, School of Education
University at Albany
Discussants—Ms. Marissa Panton and Mr. James Izzo
Graduate Students, School of Business
University at Albany
Moderator—Mr. Mark Morris

7:45–8:00p.m. ....Closing Thanks and Summary
Dr. Richard Hall

FOCUS GROUP MEETING

Professional Development of Helping Professions in Rural Communities: Trends for the 21st Century

AGENDA

November 1, 1996

8:30–9:00 a.m. .... Registration and Continental Breakfast

9:00–9:30 a.m. ....

Introductions .... Dr. Shirley Jones
Co-Chair

Greetings .... Dr. Judy Genshaft
Vice President, Academic Affairs

Greetings .... Dr. Jeanne E. Gullahorn
Vice President for Research and Graduate Studies

Greetings .... Dr. David Carpenter
Dean, School of Public Health

9:30–10:15 a.m. ....

FOCUS: Rural Health Care: A Challenge for Academic Medical Centers
Presenter—Dr. Henry Pohl
Associate Dean for Medical Education
Albany Medical College
Discussant—Mr. David Smingler
Executive Assistant to Senator Hugh Farley, NYS Senate
Moderator—Dr. Jo Ann Weatherwax

10:15–10:30 a.m. .... Break

10:30–12:00 p.m. ....

FOCUS: Economic and Social Development and Rural Social Work as a Model of the Generalist Approach for the 21st Century
Presenter—Dr. Judith A. Davenport
Professor, School of Social Work
University of Missouri, Columbia
Discussant—Dr. Anne Fortune
Acting Dean, School of Social Welfare
University at Albany

10:30–12:00 p.m. *(cont'd)*

> **FOCUS: Community-Responsive Partners for Environmental Health:**
> **Perspectives for Rural Health Professionals in the 21st Century**
> **Presenter—Ms. Lorette Picciano**, Executive Director
> Rural Coalition, Washington, DC
> **Discussant—Mr. Dwight C. Williams**
> Director of Leadership Institute
> School of Public Health, University at Albany
> **Moderator—Ms. Joan Zlotnik**

12:00–1:00 p.m. .... Lunch

1:00–2:30 p.m. ....

> **FOCUS: Strengths Perspective in Working**
> **with Families and Communities**
> **Presenter—Dr. Ann Weick**, Dean
> School of Social Welfare, University of Kansas
> **Discussant—Ms. Gloria Meert**, Program Director
> W.K. Kellogg Foundation

> **FOCUS: Public Health Collaboration and Cooperation:**
> **The Akwesasne Story**
> **Presenter—Ms. Katsi Cook**
> American Indian Program, Cornell University
> **Discussant—Dr. Lillian Brannon**, Director
> Center for Excellence in Learning and Teaching
> University at Albany
> **Moderator—Dr. Carol D. Young**

2:30–2:45 p.m. .... Break

2:45–3:30 p.m. ....

> **FOCUS: Partnerships and Collaboration Between Universities**
> **and the Communities**
> **Presenter—Dr. Katherine Briar-Lawson**, Professor
> Department of Family Studies and Social Work, Miami University, Oxford,
> Ohio
> **Discussant—Joan Sinclair**, Commissioner
> Allegany County Department of Social Services, NY
> **Moderator—Dr. Shirley Jones**

3:30–4:00 p.m. .... Wrap-up and Next Steps
Ms. Joan Zlotnik